AF447709

First published in the United States of America by:
The Evolving Nomad

To request permission please contact the publisher at:
www.theevolvingnomad.com

First Printing: June 2024
ISBN # 979-8-218-41541-9
Edited by: Bre Orcasitas
Proofread: Whitney Tayer
Cover Artwork by: Stephanie Peters
Cover Design by: James McGury
Layout by: James McGury

Disclaimer:
Some names have been changed to protect
individual's privacy. The information in this book was correct at
the time of publication, but the author does not assume any
liability for loss or damage caused by errors or omissions.

In Support of Firefighters

The fire family is just that, *family* and it's part of our
ethos to take care of one another.
With that in mind, a portion of the proceeds from
the *Hold and Improve* series will go to organizations
that assist wildland firefighters and their families
when they need it most.

Dedicated to those on our left and right in a line dig.
To our stick partners and JPs.
Our brothers and sisters.
The fire family.

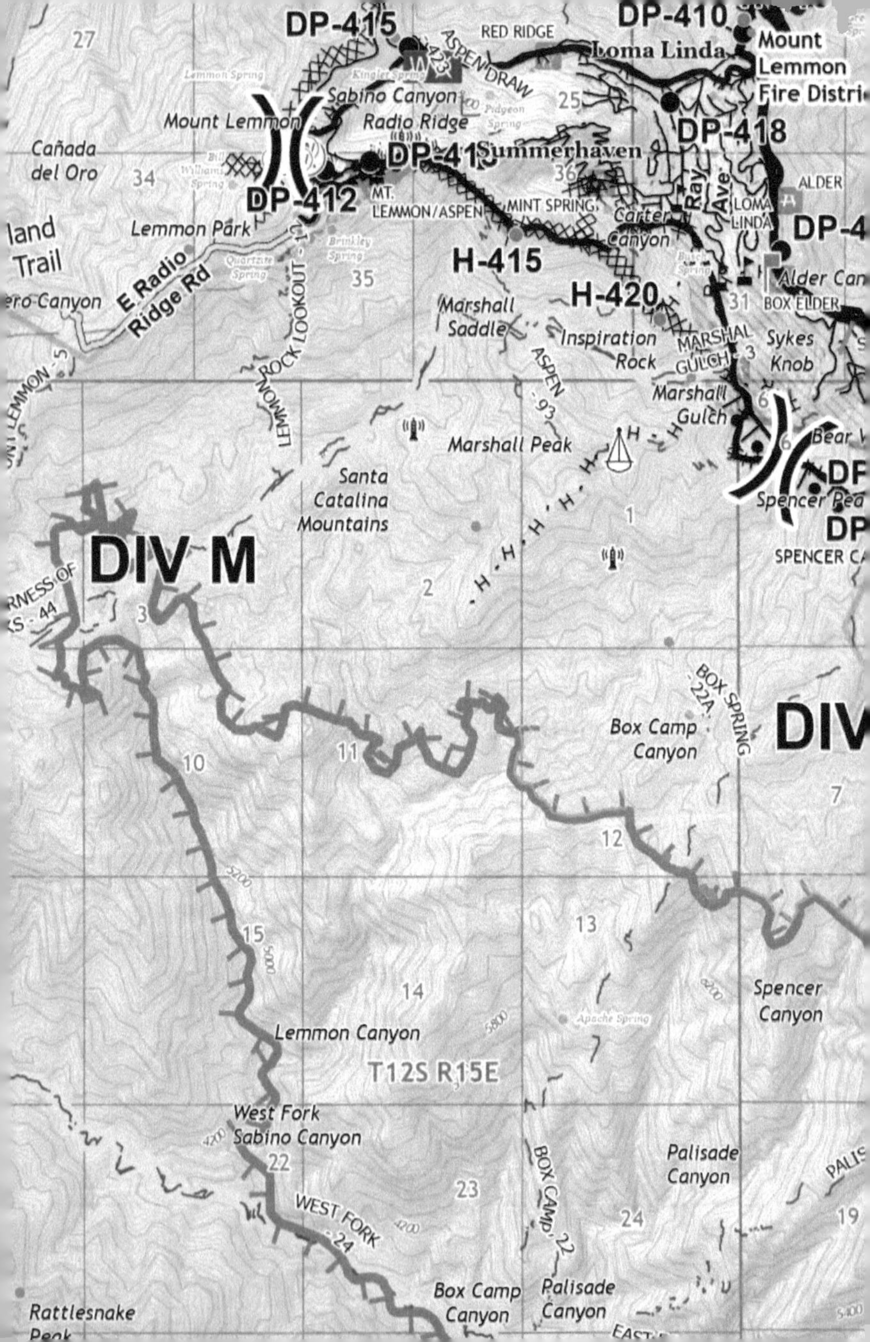

27
DP-415
RED RIDGE
DP-410
Loma Linda
Mount Lemmon Fire Distri
ASPEN DRAW
Lemmon Spring
Kinglet Spring
Sabino Canyon
Mount Lemmon
Radio Ridge
Pidgeon Spring
25
DP-418
Cañada del Oro
34
Williams Spring
DP-41
Summerhaven
36
ALDER
Ray Ave
LOMA LINDA
DP-4
DP-412
MT. LEMMON/ASPEN
MINT SPRING
Carter Canyon
Alder Can
land Trail
Lemmon Park
E Radio Ridge Rd
Brinkley Spring
BOX ELDER
ro Canyon
Quartzite Spring
35
H-415
H-420
MARSHAL GULCH 3
Sykes Knob
31
LEMMON 5
ROCK LOOKOUT 12
Marshall Saddle
Inspiration Rock
Marshall Gulch
6
Bear
DP
Spencer Pea
ASPEN 93
Marshall Peak
H H H H
H
6
DIV M
Santa Catalina Mountains
1
DP
SPENCER CA
RNESS OF S 44
2
H H H H H
Box Camp Canyon
BOX SPRING 22A
DIV
3
7
10
11
12
Box Camp Canyon
5100
13
15
5000
Spencer Canyon
14
Lemmon Canyon
5800
Apache Spring
T12S R15E
BOX CAMP
Palisade Canyon
PALIS
West Fork Sabino Canyon
420
22
23
24
19
WEST FORK 24
420
BOX CAMP 22
Rattlesnake Peak
Box Camp Canyon
Palisade Canyon
EAST

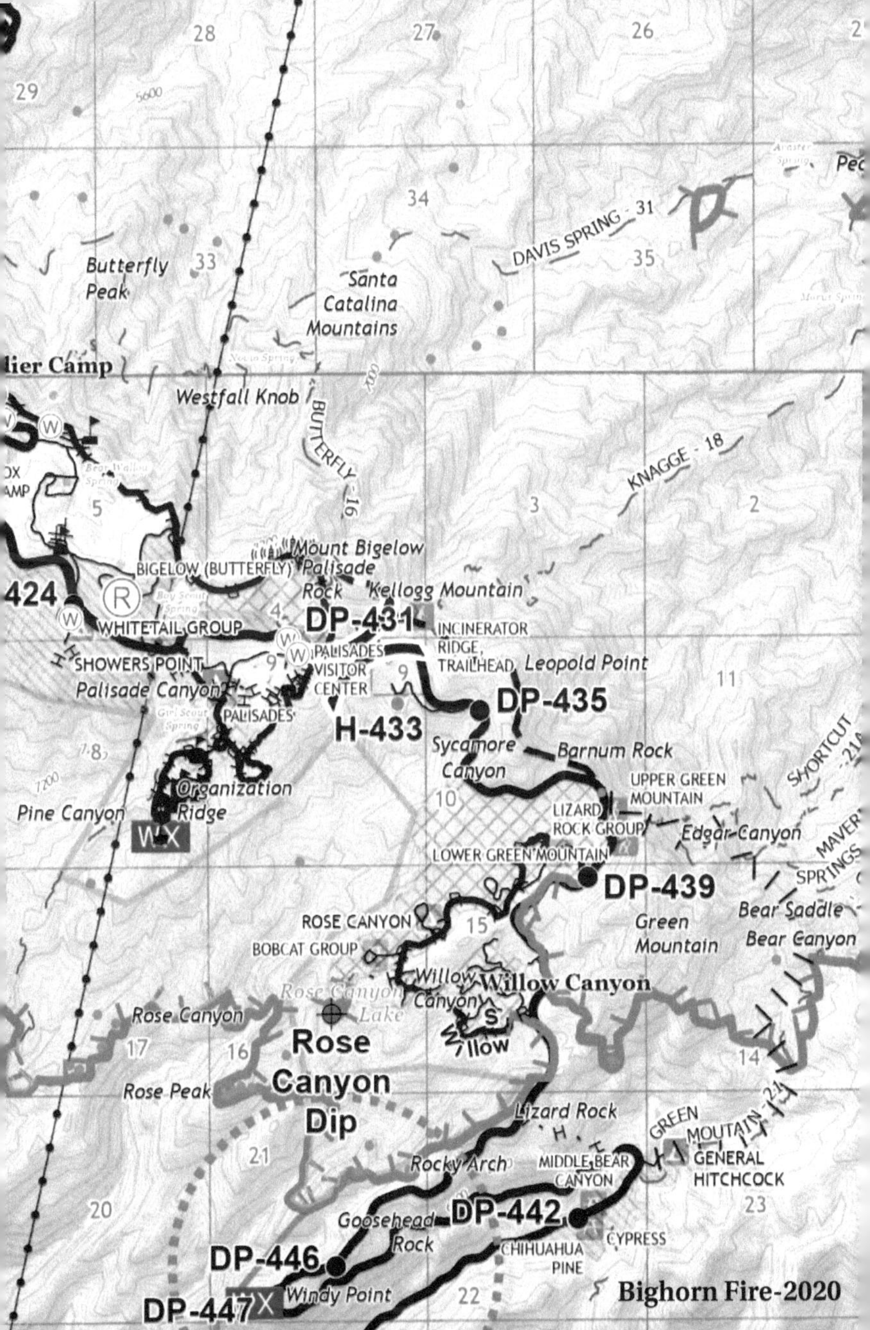
28
27
26
29
5600
Butterfly Peak
33
Santa Catalina Mountains
34
DAVIS SPRING - 31
35
Pec
dier Camp
Westfall Knob
BUTTERFLY - 16
KNAGGE - 18
3
2
W
Bear Wallow Spring
OX AMP
5
Mount Bigelow
Palisade Rock
Kellogg Mountain
BIGELOW (BUTTERFLY)
DP-431
INCINERATOR RIDGE, TRAILHEAD
Leopold Point
424
R
Boy Scout Spring
4
W
W
W
WHITETAIL GROUP
PALISADES VISITOR CENTER
9
11
SHOWERS POINT
9
DP-435
Palisade Canyon
Girl Scout Spring
PALISADES
H-433
Sycamore Canyon
Barnum Rock
SHORTCUT - 21A
7 8
7200
Organization Ridge
UPPER GREEN MOUNTAIN
Pine Canyon
10
LIZARD ROCK GROUP
Edgar Canyon
MAVER
W X
LOWER GREEN MOUNTAIN
SPRINGS
DP-439
Bear Saddle
ROSE CANYON
15
Green Mountain
Bear Canyon
BOBCAT GROUP
Willow Canyon
Willow Canyon
Rose Canyon Lake
S
illow
Rose Canyon
17
16
Rose
Canyon
Dip
14
Rose Peak
Lizard Rock
21
GREEN - 24
MOUTAIN
Rocky Arch
MIDDLE BEAR CANYON
GENERAL HITCHCOCK
20
Goosehead Rock
DP-442
23
DP-446
CYPRESS
CHIHUAHUA PINE
DP-447
X
Windy Point
22
Bighorn Fire-2020

HOLD AND IMPROVE

IMPROVE

Volume Bravo

A collection of awesomeness from
the edge of the fireline

CONTENTS

INTRODUCTION

Well, hello again all you fine people, and welcome to *Hold and Improve Volume Bravo.* I am so grateful that you're reading this introduction because that means I managed to stumble my way through the publication process not just once, but twice! Of course, as you're reading this, I'm probably face down in a puddle of drool somewhere questioning my life choices yet again, *but that's neither here nor there.*

Volume Bravo! What can I say? The fire community has stepped up to contribute an incredible collection of stories, poetry, and artwork once again. I never cease to be amazed by the fire family, and I consider it a privilege to provide a space where the fire culture can be preserved in what I consider its purest form; storytelling.

I recognize that I may be getting ahead of myself here. Surely, there are a few of you with this book in hand who haven't read *Volume Alpha,* so please allow me to back up a smidge. I'd like to include some segments of the introduction from *Hold and Improve-Volume Alpha* in order to provide you (dear appreciated reader) the full context of this book series.

Here we go...

Hold and Improve is a tribute to the fire family and our storytelling culture. What you'll find within these pages is a collection of short stories, artwork, poetry, and more. All of which, were born from the hearts, minds, and experiences of wildland firefighters. The stories shared here are relatable to a degree that it captures the essence of camaraderie on paper, while the poetry and artwork highlight the multi-faceted talents of the fire family.

The title of this book -*Hold and Improve*- is derived from the fireline. "Hold and Improve" is a familiar message passed down the line from one firefighter to the next, signifying the need to stop forward movement and improve the piece of fireline where you are. Over time, the command has also turned into a catchphrase for those moments when firefighters are sitting around staging, just waiting to engage. It's in moments like these when you might see a firefighter pull out a badly misshapen book from the depths of their line gear to help pass the time. It could be mere minutes, or several hours before being called to leap back into line order. *Hold and Improve* is comprised of short stories so that, at the very least, it gives folks a fighting chance at finishing a story before having to jump back into the fray.

I realize you may be thinking, "If this book is meant to be on the fireline, why does it have a white cover?!"

The white cover provides a blank canvas for you to leave your mark on this book. The addition of your ash-stained fingerprints is welcome and encouraged. *Hold and Improve* will not be offered in digital form because the physical experience of holding a book in your hands cannot be supplemented with a virtual substitute. And just as we share stories around the warming fire, this book can be shared too. Why not inscribe your name and the year you read it on the inside cover, then pass it off and see how far the fire world takes it?

And now I'd like to say hello and welcome, to all of you readers who aren't firefighters but have an interest in what the 'fire world' is like. *Thank you for deciding to pick up this book.* I should probably point out that the fire community more or less, has its own language and the stories within *Hold and Improve* are written as they would be told in the field. Because of this, I have provided a glossary of terms at the back of the book. This way, anyone can follow what is being said, whether or not they've ever worn fire boots. And I'm sure there are plenty of rookie firefighters who will appreciate the definitions as well.

So, there you have it, the task, purpose, and end state (leader's intent... see how I snuck that in there?) of *Hold and Improve*.

Something that I love about developing a series rather than a single book is that each volume has its own vibe; similar to when a band releases their next album. While you may notice that this volume has a couple of returning authors, the majority of *Volume Bravo* is comprised of new and different voices from the field.

I hope you enjoy *Bravo* as much as I do; and as always, a whole-hearted thank you goes out to the fire family for sending in submissions. *Hold and Improve* wouldn't exist without your contributions from the field. Thank you for helping to preserve our history and culture by sharing your stories, experiences, and talents with the world at large.

Cheers-
Bre

CHAPTER 1

THIS

Early is on time, on time is late.

Logbook for the PT hike of fire crews and local community members. Entiat, WA.

Bre Orcasitas

THE MOSAIC

My first year on a hotshot crew was hard. I spent a good portion of that fire season in survival mode, just trying to keep up with the pace of the crew. That sounds small and inconsequential, but it's not. A hotshot crew moves quickly from dawn 'til dusk. Wake up is quick, packing up sleep gear is quick, getting in/out of the rigs is quick, loading/ unloading gear is quick, eating is quick, hiking is quick, building fireline is quick... damn near everything is quick.

I was in awe of the excessively 'quick' people surrounding me. Beyond their intimidating fitness levels, their extensive knowledge about how fire moves over the landscape and fire behavior in general, was impressive. Not to mention that all these gruff, simple seeming firefighters were essentially a bunch of mini-meteorologists hiking around in the forest. That's because having the ability to do "simple things" like identify cloud types and the impending weather associated, recognize building storm cells, anticipate wind shifts, and calculate the probability of ignition all play a part in what a fire is -or is not- going to do, and knowing what a fire is going to do can be the difference between control and catastrophe.

To put it a simpler way, these people were in a long-term relationship with wildfire and I was on my 3rd date. It seemed completely outside the realm of possibility that I would ever reach the level at which they were operating. All I could do was give it everything I had each day and hope that was enough, so that's what I did.

The longer the fire season drew on, the less effort I had to put into merely surviving, and fortunately, I learned to be quick. I was still a lifetime away from the experience levels of those I was surrounded by, but I had learned a ton just by remaining observant about what was happening around me. Learning by watching became my main form of education that fire season, and for many more to come.

Staying in an observer state of mind also helped me to notice just how ritualistic and traditional the fire community is. There was most certainly a culture within the 'fire world.'

As the years passed by, and I moved between crews, I experienced fire culture from many different angles. Every crew, or geographic area, each has their own way of doing things, and traditions to uphold. Traditions that carry some sort of magical ability to bond us humans a bit closer to one another.

Depending on the crew there might be lighthearted four o'clock ice cream socials, Sunday BBQs, ping-pong championships, four-square battles, big flips, volleyball tournaments, and crew parties to partake in, because laughing together is what keeps us together.

Then there are the rituals. Rituals that you come by only when your participation in them have been earned—earned being the keyword there. This culture relies heavily upon people earning their keep, but I can attest that there isn't a much better feeling than knowing when you've earned something of your own merit, especially when it didn't come easy. Rookie helicopter rappellers have a ceremonial moment on their first operational rappel fire, as do smokejumpers on their first fire jump (If you want to know what they are, you'll have to find out the hard way). While many hotshot/hand crews bestow a crew belt buckle to deserving crewmembers. There are also esteemed awards such as "hotshot crewmember of the year" or "rookie of the year," which are typically voted on by the crewmembers rather than the overhead, making them that much more meaningful. There are plenty of traditions, rituals, and rites of passage that I've experienced which will reside in my memory, rather than on the page, because holding them close is what allows them to remain sacred.

When trying to put a finger on what it is about this profession that leaves us so closely bonded, even long after we've walked off the fireline, the root of it escapes me because it isn't any one thing. Although the traditions, rituals, and rites of passage are surely a large contributing factor, it's more than that. It's honoring the ethos of duty, respect, and integrity but it's also sleeping next to one another in the open air for months on end. It's hiking on each other's heels, and sitting together on a cliff band in comfortable silence. It's growing up, yet staying young. It's suffering together and laughing about it all later. It's a thousand shards of glass coming together to form a mosaic, and the end result is the fire family.

Julian Affuso

DÉJÀ VU

Location: Caliente, Nevada
Year: Unknown

I don't remember what year it was exactly, but I know that it had to be in the late nineties. The fire seasons of my life, which in total add up to a three-decade career, all run together in my mind. They are only marked by significant events that happened during a fire, many of which had nothing to do with the fire itself. They are also often marked by major life events at home that seem to have happened with, or without my presence. If you have a career in fire, you know what I mean. The significance of this particular story has more to do with how I was raised than the circumstances of the fire assignment, but I'll save that for later.

At the time, I was a squad boss on an Interagency Hotshot Crew based out of New Mexico, but this assignment had us rolling through Nevada from fire to fire, initial attack to initial attack, for what seemed like weeks. Most of the new starts were in the lower elevations, which meant Pinyon/Juniper and grass fires were what kept us busy. On this particular day, we were ordered to pre-position in the town of Caliente. As our crew carriers crept into town following the superintendent rig, I had the strangest feeling of deja vu come over me. I had no lucid recollection of the town itself, or when I would have been there, but it seemed familiar. As we drove the crew carrier through town my co-pilot joked that this was probably one of those towns I lived in as a kid. I laughed and joked that it was entirely possible although I didn't actually believe that to be the case, and certainly would have remembered.

We checked in with the local unit and they set us up to eat dinner. They also made a plan for us to pre-position at the elementary school where we could grab a shower and sleep in the air-conditioned gymnasium. The promise of hot food is always welcome, but the promise of cool sleeping conditions is like winning the lottery. On the first night of this particular trip, we had slept on a dirt two-track in the desert along the cool black edge of a fire that was still burning. We had been driving from our home unit back in New Mexico for what was no doubt way too many hours to meet our work-to-rest, so we needed to sleep. Why we didn't stop in Las Vegas to eat and sleep is beyond me, considering we had just driven through it two hours earlier. These are the sorts of things I question to this very day. On second thought, there are probably many good reasons why the superintendent would not want us to stay overnight in "Sin City", but I digress.

I felt a familiarity with the little town of Caliente that I chalked up to nothing more than similarities all small towns in Nevada would no doubt possess, yet the feeling nagged. As we drove to dinner, I jokingly offered directions. We would need to turn right, and then cross the railroad tracks where we'd see a local hardware store and the diner. And BAM! There it was, just as I imagined it. Then, another inexplicable moment of "knowing" happened as we drove to the school grounds. The school itself was an old white building that needed repair. I don't have any clue as to its vintage, but I imagined it had seen many generations of children and likely began its service with a very different purpose in the early part of the century. Places like that have so many stories, one of which is this one.

Growing up I had the unique opportunity to regularly travel across the western states of this beautiful country on vacation. Many of those trips ended with us living in a new town, at least for a bit. This is how I like to romanticize the reality of my childhood, but the truth is that those trips were actually not vacations at all. It seems that we moved simply for the sake of moving, or at least that was the story I told myself. As I matured, which unfortunately, happened for me and my siblings way too early, I recognized that our parents were pathological in their pursuit of freedom. Sometimes that freedom was in the form of running away from their in-laws, or in the form of the metaphorical pot of gold at the end of the rainbow. Sometimes the pursuit of freedom was literally running away in order the be free from prosecution or imprisonment. That is also a story for another time.

I spent my summers as a hotshot telling my compatriots about the time I lived in this town or that, never really getting into the specifics about why I had lived in that town or why it was only for six months. I often described my parents as bohemians or just plain old hippies. It was easier to stereotypically paint that overly simplified picture than to try and explain the truth, whatever that was. I'm not sure I myself even know the whole truth, and likely never will. Regardless, I had quite literally been down many of the roads I ended up traveling later in life as a firefighter. I had lived in many of the random places that one finds themselves in while mobilizing to fires across the mountainous west. My stories and random facts about these places entertained the crew, but mostly I was placated by the kindness of my brothers and sisters in fire. Although, my knowledge did come in handy a time or two, and I often had the benefit of providing a "local" perspective. The novelty of my life may have been interesting on its own, but honestly, I relished telling my stories because in a strange way, it brought me a feeling of acceptance. A feeling of purpose, and meaning as well, but mostly acceptance. I longed for acceptance and belonging as a child, but couldn't seem to find it because meaningful relationships don't blossom when they are torn out by the roots before they have any chance to bloom.

We finished our meal at the local diner and took showers back at the school. I could not resist calling my dad to tell him about this little town and the feelings I was having. I didn't have a cellular phone, but there was a pay phone out in front of the school, yet another reason I believe this happened in the nineties. As I described the town to my father he said in a very matter-of-fact tone, "You should recognize that school, you were in the first grade there." Well, there it was. The reason that I was feeling like I had lived there in a past life was because I had; quite literally. I prided myself on the timeline of my life, and which move led to which move. How could I have forgotten this part of my life?

I would love to end the story by saying that this was the only time I drove through a little town having lived there, with no memory of it, yet I cannot. It's happened a couple of times since, but I no longer call my father immediately, and I no longer deny the possibility that I once lived there. I just assume that it's one more place with a bit of my history. I suppose having gaps in my memory is normal, yet it's hard for me to understand. Maybe it is simply because I am human, and who really remembers everything about their childhood? Then again, there are also some good reasons why my subconscious might have chosen to forget. That is not to say my childhood was traumatic, because it wasn't. Lonely, and unconventional perhaps, but not traumatic.

The loneliness and longing for connection were what I believe led me to a career in fire, and that is the irony of it all. My childhood of nomadacy mirrors the nomadic nature of the work we do in wildland fire, but the feeling of connection I did not have as a child has been given to me in spades as an adult, and I owe that entirely to the family I have found in the fire community.

Sara Sweeney

POLLES FIRE

Location: Mazatzal Wilderness, Arizona
Year: 2020

I.

The coyotes are active this morning... the birds are just beginning their daily song as the coming sun barely tints the sky. Venus apparent, a few wispy strata-cirrus tinged with the barest of pinks. Just above the junipers clouds lurk, still hardly formed but turning orange with the impending day. Crickets make their eternal song as I begin to hear the first rustles of sleeping bags.

Next to me are the metate and grinding stone someone found yesterday, the metate smooth from years of making maize out of corn kernels, and the grinding stone perfectly balanced, smooth, finger grooves worn into it from generations of women making food for their families...

"The kind of thing that was passed from mother to daughter," he had said.

And I can see a young woman ready to begin making her own home and family, holding it reverently along with her memories as her mother gifts it to her, not needing to explain its importance or meaning. A ritual passed down, enacted by so many generations of mothers and daughters, no matter which continent or culture or era they lived in... this one happened to be here on this mesa in the desert Southwest, and here it will stay.

And how lucky we are to be a part of it, for even a short time.

Echo Cunningham

SALT//ASH

everything that happens
        here
i carry with me.

i catch your laugh on the
        wind,
remember what
           color
the sky was that night—

blue-black
      iridescent
      stars
salt-lamp orange lines of fire in the
fading
light.

we howl like wolves
      wild
essence nature exposed

both the sacred
and
the mundane
lead to this.

eyes
          always
                    open
gathering the dust from
our footsteps as evidence
          as artifact—

listen,
          when you took me under your wing
i grew into my own.

Jamie Strelnik

MY LAST SUPPER

Location: Clear Creek Complex. Salmon-Challis, Idaho.
Year: 2000

It was the year 2000, and my rookie season as a hotshot on a crew based out of Montana. My first two years as a firefighter were slow, which meant that I saw very little fire. Instead, I learned how to build split-rail fences when we weren't driving around for hours, in a cramped engine, looking for elusive lightning strike fires in Northern Washington. All this meant that I truly had no idea what I was getting myself into by signing onto a hotshot crew, I was in for a rude awakening.

For one thing, the amount of weight on our backs was no less than forty-five pounds, often more, along with carrying whatever equipment and supplies were needed for twenty people to complete a shift. Chainsaw fuel, drip torches, medical equipment, and cubees were often carried along just in case we got low on drinking water, or we needed to burn out a section of ground. As a rookie, you often end up carrying the extra supplies. In fact, if you're a smart rookie you will volunteer to carry whatever is needed without complaint, you just do it.

You could say that hotshots are "what if" kinda folks. They're handy to have around when problems need solving, or if there's an insane amount of work that needs doing on very little sleep; call a hotshot.

But as I said, I was a rookie, not yet a real hotshot. I was opinionated, stubborn, not in "hotshot shape," and way more confident in my abilities than I should have been. At first, I did what any typical human would do, I didn't volunteer to carry more weight in the hopes that I would be able to keep up with the hiking and work pace. That plan definitely didn't make me any friends. I was not what you'd call a shining star kinda rookie!

One day our crew got an assignment for the Clear Creek Complex. Just before we loaded up and took off, my friend who was a rookie on a hotshot crew based in New Mexico called to check in and see how I was doing. He offered me some advice.

He said, "Volunteer for everything, be the first to stand, the last to sit down, and don't speak unless spoken to."

He had been in the military prior to becoming a firefighter and had already graduated from the school of hard knocks.

We arrived at the fire camp for the Clear Creek Complex in the evening. It was an iconic spot for a fire camp, located between the old Indianola Rappel Base, and the North Fork Ranger Station on the Salmon River in Idaho. It was also one of the only flat spots in that entire canyon, which consists mainly of incredibly steep terrain. And there I sat, on the ground in my oversized Nomex pants, a new maroon hotshot t-shirt, and my stiff logger-style fire boots. I remember that it was almost dark, and a beautiful evening. It was warm, with a summer breeze blowing through the canyon. I stared intently at the steepness surrounding me while eating what felt like my last supper; which was an MRE of all things.

I was sure I was going to wash out the next day! Washing out basically means failing miserably and quitting either by the leadership's strong encouragement or by your own shame. I pulled my boots off and patched my blistered feet as I continued to stare across the Salmon River at the mountains we were going to climb at Mach 10 speed the next morning. To make matters worse, there were several hotshot crews who would be working with us, and hotshots enjoy nothing more than some friendly competition.

Earlier that day, someone had made the remark, "Hotshot Olympics here we come!"
And another person yelled, "You're not a hotshot until you fight fire on the Salmon-Challis!"

I didn't really understand what that meant yet, but it sounded horrible. For one, on my best day, I'm not Olympic material. And two, I was one of less than a handful of women on all the combined hotshot crews assigned to this fire. There were dudes for days!

Finally, I choked down my MRE, gingerly put my fire boots back on, and crawled into my sleeping bag fully dressed. You might be wondering why someone would sleep with their clothes and boots on. When you have about three minutes from the wake-up call to get dressed, put your sleeping bag away, and be ready to go to work, you just stay dressed.

I spent most of the night lying in my sleeping bag, feeling terrified that I would fall out of the hike the next day. The concern about falling out of hikes was not new for me, and neither was losing sleep over it, but this night in particular, I did something besides panic. I visualized myself hiking with the crew and getting to the familiar point where it felt like there was no oxygen making it to my limbs, and that I couldn't take another step. Right at that moment, I would visualize that I kept going instead of stopping. I did this over and over again. I had also decided to take my buddy's advice. After all, I didn't have a friend on the crew, I might as well work hard and be quiet.

The next thing I knew, I was being woken up by my squad boss shaking my sleeping bag. I leapt up, and started stuffing my sleeping bag in my overnight bag before I was even fully coherent. No time to consider what I was going to do that day, just go! After that, we all made our way down to the river where an older, quiet gentleman sat waiting for us in a canoe. Two at a time, we were being rowed across the river to begin our work. It was all I could do to force myself into the canoe, feeling sure that this was going to be my last day as a hotshot. If only he could row slower! But there I was on the other side, taking my place in line order, waiting to begin the hike from hell.

I became a hotshot on the Salmon-Challis during that roll. I learned that being a hotshot was physical, but even more so, it was mental. We ended up spending twenty-one days hiking and digging handline on those steep slopes. There were times when the fire behavior got too intense, or lightning chased us off the mountain, but we'd always hike back up again, much to my dismay.

I would be on that crew for the next three years, and the friendships that grew in those years remain today. My rookie season shaped me as a leader. I learned how to use my weaknesses and turn them into strengths. It also gave me patience and humor for new firefighters learning physical and mental toughness. What matters most is that a new firefighter comes in willing to learn, and has a good attitude. It also doesn't hurt to sit down last, get up first, and always be willing to volunteer.

Years later I led a twenty-person hand crew up those same mountains on the other side of the river, breathing hard and with a smile on my face, thinking back to my rookie hotshot season. And let me tell you, being in the front of a hike is far easier than being in the back!

A graduate of Hotshot Hard Knocks University,
Jamie Strelnik

Rita Chandler

ANGEL IN WHITES

From a firefighting mother to her firefighting daughter.

She wears such small boots to carry the heavy load,
From early morning into the night.
Yet she works with a smile digging the line.
I call her my Angel in Whites.

Her small hands in leather gloves covered in ash,
Work the Pulaski as she holds on tight.
The crew calls her part of Squad B....
I call her my Angel in Whites.

Her soft brown hair tucked hidden beneath her hardhat,
That protects her when things don't go just right.
She gives this job her very best effort.
I call her my Angel in Whites.

Dressed in green and yellow like nineteen others,
She is here on the fireline to fight.
As a crew, not a war, but the flames.

I call her my Angel in Whites.

Keep this girl safe Lord and guide her,
I pray with all my might.
I trust that you'll watch over
My Angel in Whites.

CHAPTER 2
Beautiful Suffering

"People don't put out fires, coffee and batteries put out fires."

– Sarah Brown

Crew PT hike, logbook entry. Entiat, WA.

Quin Anderson

THE SHARP ROCK FIRE

Location: Sharp Rock Fire, Oregon
Year: 2009

It was an early July smoke report in what would end up
being a pretty tame fire season. A small lightning bust
had passed through and hit a few areas in the high country of our district up along the crest. The Bravo squad
of our crew was tasked with a new start in a remote and
difficult part of the Mount Washington Wilderness. After
several hours of walking and falling, through a wall of
thick ten-foot-tall rhododendron, we arrived at what
would be our new home for the next couple of shifts.

The fire was two miles off from the initial smoke report location, which ended up changing our suppression plan.
We thought this fire was going to be lakeside, but the reality was that the nearest pond was a mile-and-a-half away,
with a tricky lava field to navigate. In fact, the fire itself
was smack dab in the middle of the lava field in a deca-
dent timber stringer, and the fire was burning in four-to-

six-foot DBH dead and down trees. Bravo squad dug-in knowing that this was going to be a dry mop show with no soil to use in the middle of a lava field, and only two bladder bags to work with.

By the end of the first shift, we had the fire lined. But as we prepared to bed down for the night, we began to realize there wasn't any good spot to do it. People awkwardly perched themselves up around dead logs and large trees. Everyone got a comfy three-to-five minutes of rest before the mosquitoes and ants began to strike. All night we endured the incessant whine and bite of every bug on the mountain crest. The only solitude where we could escape it was in the thick smoke coming off of the burning dead and down trees.

Shift number two was a water run. Two folks from the squad took both of the bladder bags and began the long slog to the nearest water source a mile-and-a-half away. The other three from Bravo squad bucked, scraped, and burned the heavy fuels of the fire. Upon arrival back to our little camp, the two who'd gone for water informed the rest of the group that the water filters were either missing from our pumps or had molded, which meant the water we had to drink was going to be risky. As thirsty as we all were, we drank it anyway and saved the rest of the pond water to throw on the fire.

At one point, I remember looking up to see our sawyer running the chainsaw at maximum RPMs -not moving- just standing there with the saw at full bore. I watched him for a couple of minutes before I had him shut down his saw and told him to grab some shade and take a break. During my hike back to camp the rhododendron grabbed hold of my pants, ripping them from ankle to crotch, thus allowing every bug in the wilderness full access.

Looking around at the squad on our third shift was a sight. They didn't even twitch as mosquitoes covered their faces, and ants dangled from their ears and lips. They all had dead eyes looking nowhere. No words were spoken as everyone suffered together in complete silence. I have no doubt tears would have been shed if anyone had a thimble's worth of moisture left in their bodies.

In the midst of all this, we received a weather update that a wet, cold front was moving in and that we needed to get out before it hit. This was welcome news that would finally put us out of our misery. Our hike out ended with us re-entering civilization through a campground. I watched as mothers pulled their children in close, ushering them to safety, which is fair; we looked like the walking dead.

We spent shift number four down at the clinic, where we all got medication for Giardia.

To all the ones who were there... holy shit!

Andrew Mattox

THE FEW. THE PROUD. THE LOST.

In the flames with America's finest.
And in the brush.
And in the river...

Location: Buck Creek, Washington
Year: 2004

"Yeah," I said into my 2-way radio, *"Buck Creek is basically impassable."*

"Impossibly impassable! I heard you say it plain as day!" Kelly would object years later, contesting the facts. His wife tried not to laugh in her beer as his voice elevated to a squealing mockery, "Buck Creek is impooooossibly impaaaasssssable!"

"What!?" I objected. *"I'd never say something as stupid as that!"*

"Oh, you said it, Lockjaw!" Kelly exclaimed.

That's me: *Lockjaw. Crash. The Stuttering Monkey.* There's

a secret language in the jump world, full of tough-guy names like "Viper" and "Wolfman," only they all sound more like "Lunchbox," "Smellsby," and "Chickenhawk."

Kelly Barbarous, the Basque redneck of Burns, Oregon, had not been embracing towards me. He was the sort of high-price character who willingly jumped out of moving airplanes over the North Cascade mountains, and had been doing it for nearly a decade. I was a rookie and had just earned my wings. Kelly had only repeated two words to me all fire season.

Whenever I passed by him, I'd say, *"Hi Kelly."*

With dark sunglasses, a clipped goatee, and broad shoulders that were home to a black *Ramones* t-shirt, he'd give a surly grunt and mutter, "Hey man."

I wondered if he'd ever warm up to me. You know, *smile.*

I was based out of "the smokejumper base that time forgot." The oldest, the smallest, and perhaps the most whacked-out jump base in the U.S.A. It's like a family. *A crime family.* Mixed with Fleetwood Mac.

Our base manager is like the Don. Rookies are the runners. Senior jumpers are the enforcers. Squad leaders;

the made men. Sphinx McWhisperman, our loft foreman and the longest-serving jumper in the world was the quiet Godfather.

Now, 2,000 vertical feet of the conifer-clad mountain below me, Kelly, and the Puerto Rican Chickenhawk heard me loud and clear.

I, the squeaky little runner, just told a couple of scarface thugs that something was impossible.

"Impassable? Does he know what we go through?"

They were not amused.

Eight of us had jumped this small isolated fire together, six miles up the precipitous valley of Buck Creek near Darrington, Washington. Crashing down into a series of avalanche meadows nearly 2,000 vertical feet above our fire, that landing taught me that my body can bounce.

This fire wasn't too remote as far as smokejumper fires go, but it was remote enough. Welcome to the North Cascade mountains of Washington State's Westside. Westside is an important but subtle distinction from Eastside in the North Cascades. It's like the difference between a tea poodle and a hyena. The Eastside has dry, stately Ponderosa pine glades and flowery, nymph-infested meadows. The Westside is the forestry equivalent of the wrong end of a prison riot. The terrain is carved into a labyrinth of gorges, choked in tangled slide alder and shaded by gloomy fir canopies. When ultra-light hikers die after lives ill-spent, the unluckiest souls are to be sent to an untrailed version of the Westside of the North Cascades to atone for their sins, while the others merely go to hell.

Being the rookie in the group, I was given helicopter duty. I stayed at the jump spot bagging our jump gear, waiting to sling it out under a helicopter. The ship didn't arrive until the next day, so I had time to admire the view, and... wait. That's when I realized, I'd been here before.

I recognized the ridges across the valley. I was there just 3 months prior, training for my rookie season by beating the stuffing out of myself in the backcountry. I knew exactly where we were.

"Ooooooohhhh, we're up THAT Buck Creek." We all gonna die.

I hadn't actually ventured into Buck Creek on my insane little training journey. No, no. The closest I'd gotten was a chilling view downslope, and colorful prose from two of my friends who described their attempt to go up Buck

Creek in terms usually reserved for European armies conducting winter invasions of Russia. These two friends subsequently walked from Seattle to the Aleutian Islands and described much of that trip as "fun."

"Ha ha ha!" we'd all laughed, "pity the poor sucker who gets stuck up Buck Creek!"

As I waited for a helicopter, I contemplated this. Radio traffic cropped up between my compatriots and dispatch, discussing the merits of going out the creek bottom. That's when I keyed the microphone, disconnected my brain from my voice box, and perhaps changed the psyches of Kelly and Chickenhawk forever.

"Buck Creek is basically impassable."

Nearly a day later – and 14 hours after uttering those ill-considered words – I hooked our net-wrapped jump gear onto a hundred-foot steel cable swaying beneath a Bell 206 helicopter in the early-morning light. As it soared away, I shouldered my rucksack and set off down the steep chutes and gullies, tracking my way to the fire.

I reached the others by 8:00 a.m. They'd reduced the fire to a swath of mud and sodden brush surrounding the blackened, flame-hollowed hulk of an enormous old-growth

Douglas fir log. Everyone had packed up their equipment into their rucksacks, ready to start thrashing toward the nearest road.

Kelly and Chickenhawk, forming the self-appellated *"Latin Team One,"* already had their rucksacks on, ready to roll. They didn't talk to me; my comments did not merit acknowledgement. My rookie-ness had affronted the rugged, never-say-die esprit of the jump base. Within fifteen minutes they were gone into the brush, bound for glory out the bottom of Buck Creek.

"So, Mattox, what do you know about Buck Creek?" Nancy "Jackie O" Floyd asked after *Latin Team One* had left.

Jackie is a smart one – and the only other person whose real name I use in this story, presumably because she is the only one of us not currently being hunted by federal agents.

"Well," I admitted, *"It's not technically impassable. It just takes ass-kicking very seriously."*

Hours later, we got a scratchy radio contact from *Latin Team One*. Something about "slow going." Then... nothing.

By noon, Jackie and two boosters from Oregon had taken my casual descriptions of being throttled by homicidal vegetation into account. They set out, climbing up toward the naked ridge crests over 2,500 vertical feet above us, seeking to escape the valley by crossing the mountains amid remnant snowfields.

Myself and two others were left to wait for the helicopter to sling out the pump and hoses. Those two were Oregonite smokejumper Moose Biggie and *The Woz.*

Returning to the Mafia model; the Woz was the operations foreman at the base. The hard-nosed Capo of our little world. Short, broad, and florid. A man who once appeared in a pickup truck advertisement, and happened to be physically present when the unfortunate act of blowing up a beached whale with dynamite happened along the shoreline of Florence, Oregon.

The Woz flies his parachute like a demolition derby driver and has got a *really* good landing roll.

"My strategy," he explains, "is to turn into a bowling ball. You ever see a bowling ball dropped from 1,500 feet? You could probably still bowl with that thing."

The Woz wasn't hearing any of this *over-the-ridge* crap.

"Hell," he cheerfully exclaimed, "I just want to see how bad it really is."

Like Tom Cruise at the end of *Top Gun,* flying his F-14 Tomcat alongside rival "Iceman" versus the faceless commie MiG-flying baddies, I had to stick with the Woz.

I will not leave my ops foreman! I chanted to myself over and over, amid riffs of big-guitar music going off in my brain. *I'm going to earn my hazard pay, dammit!*

Then I had an ominous thought; what if things get ugly on the hike out? Who would get eaten for food? I looked at Moose; he was a big guy. Big. The smoke-jumping champion of both SPAM and moose-meat eating. I looked back at the Woz, the human wrecking ball. Then I looked down at myself, weighing in at 158 pounds. *Rookie... Hmmm, I could see where this was going.* I considered drinking some pump fuel to spoil my meat but decided to take my chances.

As we waited for the ship to arrive, the Woz regaled me with tales of the old days. Apparently, the 2x4 drawbar with steel brackets bolted across the door to my room in the bunkhouse was something he and his roommates installed during their rookie season, 20-some years ago. The older jumpers would come home from the bar every night and beat the crap out of the rookies.

"Only reason I stayed," the Woz explained, "was I didn't have any place to go back to." After Woz & Co. installed the "rookie bar," the old guys ran a fire hose through the attic, hooked it up to the jump base's water system, and opened the valves.

"Yeah," the Woz said. "That didn't go over well. The old base manager had to crack down after that."

If I had any doubts about my rookie year of scrubbing toilets and occasionally getting called "rook," they were dispelled. Life in 2004 was good, even though I was going to pull the short straw and get eaten halfway down Buck Creek.

The helicopter we heard thumping up the canyon to sling out our cargo was a hopped-up Hughes 500; a bastard hybrid of a chicken egg, a dragonfly, and a whole lot of methamphetamines. Yet with it came providence. The man at the stick was Birdman; *The* Birdman. His name is changed here. I couldn't get consent to use it if I tried; I never even knew his full name. I didn't need to know it, because he's a mythical character – like Gandalf, or Prince. He was a private contractor renowned in our neck of the Cascades as a rotor-wizard who – as lore would have it – built his first helicopter at home and learned to fly it by slinging cedar logs out of mountain gorges.

Pulling out our pump cargo now, on a 100-foot steel cable, his voice crackled over the radio: "Anything else I can do for you boys?"

"Yeah," the Woz joked into the mic, "how about a lift home?"

There was a momentary pause. "Sure. There's a gravel bar about a half-mile downstream I can land in. If you're there when I get back, I'll take you home."

The Woz looked at us. We looked at him.

"We'll be there!" the Woz exclaimed. Then he grabbed his rucksack and hurled himself off the mountain.

In hot pursuit, I plunged after him. Hurtling down 100%+ slopes, bouncing from tree to tree, I realized something as the Woz vanished into the distance; the Woz goes through the woods exactly like he jumps out of an airplane. When I finally caught up to him after a quarter-mile of a controlled free-fall, he was waist-deep in the creek bottom pushing through salmonberry bushes, grinning and bleeding out his forehead.

"I jumped over a log," he shouted. "And there was nothing there! I slid headfirst down the slope – good thing there was a tree there to stop me. That tree saved my life!"

Moose came trundling downslope after us idiots, shaking his head. We all charged downstream, bashing through the thickets.

Birdman deftly maneuvered into the hellhole and plucked us to freedom, jet turbines screaming at full power, with the grace of a psychotic ballerina wielding twin samurai swords. As we soared up the mountain slopes, crammed inside the fiberglass egg of the ship's fuselage, I looked down Buck Creek's axe cleft through the mountains. Moose shook his head. The Woz mouthed something that looked like "not good."

It called to mind Jesse Ventura's line in *Predator,* "You lose it out there, you'd be in a world of shit."

Two hours later, after a mountain-jumping helicopter flight and a van ride to the mouth of Buck Creek, I hiked up a fisherman's trail looking for Latin Team One. After a quarter-mile, the trail abruptly ended. The rocky canyon walls came together in a rocky V of foaming whitewater, slopes tangled with moss, dwarf hemlock, and spindly cedar.

I keyed my radio, "Puerto Rico- *Mattox"* I called. Nothing. "Puerto Rico- *Mattox."* Nothing.

Huh. Six miles? Well... six miles can't be too bad, can it? True, Kelly and Chickenhawk. are, uh... Hell magnets. But...well surely, I mean...

I broke down; please, please, please let it be *Chickenhawk who comes out first!*

Then I noticed movement in the brush. Some crashing, some cussing, and a staggering motion.

Kelly emerged, half-climbing through the tangled vegetation, clinging to the steep rock; eyes glazed with a 1,000-yard stare. He staggered to a stop, as his head swiveled in my direction ever so slowly. The spirit world faded from his sight as his eyes focused in like a giant squid sighting a scuba diver. *Uh oh.* I braced for it.

The sporadic testimonials of Kelly's 11.5 hours in Buck Creek, and Chickenhawk's 12.5 hours of fighting through a semi-vertical carnage of broken logs, cliff bands, and interwoven salmonberry are - to this day – difficult to decipher, especially through all the cussing. With light packs, superb training, and plenty of chew, they still averaged a speed of only ½ mile per hour. Chickenhawk reported that he walked– or climbed – until he fell into the snowmelt river, then he'd float until he hit shore and repeat *ad nauseum.*

Kelly remembers Chickenhawk floating past him at one point and shouting, *"What the hell are you doing, Chickenhawk?"*

"Don't ever fucking do that! Why'd you have to say *impassable?"* He howled, his voice registering at a shrill soprano.

"You could've said, only an idiot would go out that creek! Or, it's pure hell in there!" And we'd have understood; why did you have to say *IMPASSABLE!?!"*

Kelly and I have been friends ever since. Those halcyon days of SPAM and hoses are behind me now, and I have tried unsuccessfully to integrate into Western civilization.

People ask me what I miss. "Is it the excitement? The danger?"

Or is it Jackie, half charming- half strong-arming me, into singing *Paradise City* by Guns 'N' Roses in a Darrington karaoke bar?

No, I say. *It's the people.*

Willow Merritt

MISERABLE FUN

Location: Tennessee
Year: 2017

The year was 2017, and I was working on a hotshot crew based out of North Carolina. We had gotten called to Tennessee to help out with a prescribed fire that was set to burn about 1,000 acres. Our crew was in charge of lighting the blackline at the top of the burn, and then holding the fireline as we lit to ensure we didn't get any spot fires.

One specialized piece of equipment essential to firefighting in the southeastern part of the United States is a trusty backpack leaf blower. Since the majority of the fuel in that region is leaf litter, using a leaf blower makes getting down to mineral soil about three times faster than digging by hand. My truck mate Mitchell had been running the leaf blower for several days, so I volunteered to take it for this Rx burn.

We got shuttled up to the top of the burn unit by an ATV and I went to work with the other squad's leaf blower operator, re-clearing the fireline of any leaf litter. One of the main things about running a leaf blower is that they are really loud. It's very difficult to hear your radio, so I actually had no idea the Rx burn had even started until a crewmember came and tracked me down.

The wind was pushing hard across the fireline, making spot fires inevitable. So little 5'3" me, wearing my line gear with a backpack leaf blower stacked on top (sitting pretty much over my head), started running back toward the start of the burn to assist. Once the first spot fire was extinguished, I took a breath and shut down the leaf blower. As it turns out this was an untimely mistake, because all of a sudden, I heard "spot fire!" announced over the radio, and so off I went! Smoke was rolling across the line, thick, heavy, and acrid, which made running while simultaneously trying not to choke on smoke nearly impossible. Luckily, I wear contact lenses, which helped to seal my eyes from the awful effects of smoke exposure, however, some of my comrades were not so lucky.

When I arrived at the next spot fire, Mitchell was quite literally a hot mess of snot and red weeping eyes, to the point that he could barely see. Breathless I shouted, "Start me up, Mitchell!" I held steady as he fumbled through teary eyes, finally landing on the pull cord, and after a couple of good tugs, the leaf blower sprang back to life. Another spot fire caught, and then another one radioed in! This went on for a few hours. Eventually, I caught a break and got switched out with the other squad's leaf blower operator who had missed the whole episode by being assigned to blow the fireline out ahead of us. We switched places and I bumped ahead still blowing away, but it was a nice respite from running through smoke. The crew finally got a break late in the day to grab some food and sit for a minute, and it was clear that we were all beat. I felt like an 80-year smoker with emphysema from all the oak smoke I had inhaled by the end of the whole ordeal.

We didn't get the burn completed that day, and we spent the next day chasing after more spot fires, but it is a memory I look back on with fondness. Embracing the suck, literally, all of us together. *What miserable fun.*

Hanne Beener

THE HORSE

Location: Central Washington
Year: 2010

It was a hot summer day under a clear blue sky; *August 6th* to be exact. I remember the date vividly because it was the day my best friend's daughter was born; a birth I missed, because a three-pronged bolt of lightning winged out of a clear blue sky and startled a whole lot of random people who share parts in this story.

I was on the ready load that morning at my rappel crew's home base in Eastern Washington. I remember feeling pretty nonchalant about being first-up because there was nothing of significance in the fire weather forecast. So, of course, we got a fire call for a smoke report. The four of us, two locals and two boosters, were all curious whether there would actually be anything at the coordinates we'd received from dispatch.

As we flew overhead we spotted two definitive smokes,

and then we saw... *horses running through the smoking trees?* The third thing we noticed was a bunch of abandoned gear that was on the verge of being burned over.

Ah, we thought knowingly, *people doing stupid things in the woods again!*

We could not have been more wrong.

The four of us split into two sticks. I was to be the ICT5 trainee assigned to the smoke on the ridge along with my stick partner, while the other two went mid-slope to assess the second smoke. The rappel from the helicopter was uneventful, but as the two of us approached the fire, we began to hear the sound of an animal in distress. Before long we saw a mule tied to a tree not too far from the leading edge of the fire. It was laden with saddle packs and pulling as hard as it could to escape.

Upon seeing this we did some further scene assessment. There were several saddle packs strewn about, half-eaten lunches scattered across the ground, and lots of riding helmets. *Child-sized riding helmets.* But there were no children or humans of any size for that matter. With sinking stomachs and sweaty palms, we weren't sure what to think.

The fire had been more active when we observed it from the air, but the fire behavior mellowed enough for us to get close and peer through the smoke at the interior. It was then that we caught a glimpse of it. The ass-end of a dead packhorse, which was tied to a smoking tree. I don't remember who said it, but one of us looked at the other and said, 'I think that horse got struck by lightning and started the fire.'

I radioed dispatch to give the initial size up but mentioned nothing about the horse, assuming there were many eager ears listening to the radio traffic on what should have been an uneventful day. Instead, I pulled out my phone which miraculously had service but was nearly out of battery life.

I called the dispatch center and said, *"This is the IC trainee from Incident #XXX, and I need to fill you in on a developing situation,"* and then my phone died.

Not wanting to leave dispatch hanging, I meekly asked my stick partner to borrow his phone. Reconnected, I filled dispatch in,

"It appears that lightning struck a packhorse–yes, a horse. It was part of a group of at least five young riders based on the equestrian helmets found at the scene. No. There are no human casualties in the fire area, but we don't know where

they are, or how they are. Do you want us to find people or put the fire out? Oh, and there's a mule tied up that is alive. Oh, and also, we just saw a new smoke pop up across the valley from where we are, on the opposite ridge. You should send another load of rappellers out here."

Dispatch replied to all of this with, "We'll call you back."

While we waited, we triple-checked that there were in fact, no fatalities other than the horse. We noticed a well-maintained backcountry trail that the packtrain must have been using, so my stick partner jogged down the path a bit to see if he could find anyone while I knocked down the flames that were nearing the frantic mule. We got the go-ahead from dispatch to engage the fire and were told that the Sheriff's office had been alerted to look for the missing people in question. Fortunately, it didn't take us long to get a containment line around the fire, which was under a quarter of an acre in size.

As we worked piling up all the fuel to the fire's interior, we couldn't help but stare at the horse, which at this point was wafting a strong cooked animal smell. We decided we'd try and pile everything onto the horse in an attempt to get it to fully consume. After getting a red-hot funeral pyre going, we moved on to engage with the mule.

Neither of us had any experience with pack animals or equines in general, so we made sure to approach with caution. The mule kicked and bucked wildly so we retreated. Eventually, enough mutual, and tenuous trust was built for us to untie the saddle packs and give it more lead so it could lie down, but we left it tied up since the fire danger had been eliminated.

The riders from the packtrain were located about three hours later and all were accounted for. While we were still awfully curious about what had happened, that was a good enough ending for the day. We retreated to our camp further along the ridgeline, where we met up with eight other rappellers who had all been busy tackling their own new fire starts that day.

Unfortunately, the next morning we came to find that the funeral pyre we had built was unsuccessful. The horse had not been fully consumed by the fire; far from it actually. We begrudgingly worked around the horse's remains until about midday, when two women suddenly appeared at the fire's edge.

It quickly became clear to us that they were the distraught owners of the pack animals. As tactfully as we could, we explained the situation. They thanked us and said their farewells to Tess the horse before sadly leading the mule down the trail.

After they left, we hot-spotted the fire then cold trailed, giving the horse as wide of a berth as possible. By the end of shift, the cooked meat smell from the day before had transitioned into the unmistakable scent of death and decay, and we were more than happy to be done for the night. Back at camp, someone heated up a broccoli cheddar freeze dried meal and my stick partner and I both began gagging and swearing. If you were ever wondering what a two-day-gone horse smells like, it's that exact freeze-dried meal scent.

Later, while we sat relaxing around our cooking fire, we were suddenly surprised by a young man who nervously stepped out of the shadows and identified himself as the leader of the packtrain that had gone missing the day prior. He explained that he and nine kids had stopped on the ridge for lunch during a multi-day pack trip from a nearby dude ranch. He then told us how out of a clear blue sky, a three-pronged lightning bolt cracked into the basin where we were. Tess the horse, was killed instantly while almost as instantly, the grove of trees where she was tied up, caught fire. The chaperone quickly led the kids down the trail a safe distance, then ran back to cut the other horses loose. However, in all the chaos, he had missed releasing the mule. He hiked the kids down to the closest trailhead

where they found law enforcement waiting. He nervously handled a tin cup that he'd recovered from the fire as
he expressed that the kids were quite distraught over the
whole thing. Understandably, he seemed fragile and sad
about it all. We wished him well and then he disappeared
into the night.

The next day, we were back on the fire for more cold trail-
ing, still avoiding Tess as best we could. With the scent of
death still wafting, we decided that we'd had quite enough
of this incident, and began our six hour watch. At one
point, I left the fire's edge and wandered into the bushes
to go pee, when all of a sudden, I came face to face with
a man holding a gun. He explained that he'd heard there
was a dead horse nearby and figured that would attract
bears, so he was there to do some bear hunting. A bit un-
easy about his presence, I said he could post up far away
from us. Later, we wondered whether what he was doing
was even legal.

The afternoon dragged on. It was hot, and the stench of
poor Tess became overpowering to the point that my stick
partner finally lost it. He sprang up from a prone position,
grabbed a combi-tool, and began flinging dirt at the horse,
cussing all the while. He spent up his energy and yet the
horse still remained. Just then, from out of nowhere, a
young girl and boy appeared right next to us. We sheep-

ishly wondered if they had heard the outburst.

"Whatcha doing?" asked the girl, who was about eight.

We explained the situation and then asked, *"Are you two out here by yourselves? Where are your parents?"*

"We're mostly by ourselves," the boy said casually. "Our dad's out here bear hunting, but we haven't seen him for hours."

They stuck around for a while but eventually grew bored and wandered down the trail. Not long after that, we were jolted by the sound of screaming. My stick partner and I locked eyes, both of us with nerves frayed by a constant barrage of stressful oddities on this fire. I headed down in the direction of the screaming and came upon a large group of ladies hiking up the trail. I asked if they were okay, and whether they'd heard the screaming. They confirmed they were fine and hadn't heard anything so I continued on hiking for another mile or so down the trail, calling out to see if I could get a response from anyone. I returned just as my stick partner was finishing up a question-and-answer session with the women's hiking group about the odd circumstances of the fire. It didn't take long for them to retreat due to the stench.

Our six hour watch finished up right around dusk, but not before a second encounter with the alleged bear hunter, who came strolling by with his kids in tow. Everyone seemed okay, or at least they said they were when we asked them. We thought it best to keep our conversation short and tried not to let our unease show.

I called dispatch to let them know I was calling the fire out and that we'd be hiking off in the morning even though Tess was still there, and still stinky, but at least she was cold. We happily fled the fireline toward camp, trying in vain to clear the smell of dead horse from our nostrils.

On the hike out the next day, I enjoyed the fresh clean air by the lungful as we made our way through flowered meadows and along a creek, which led to the trailhead. As I hiked along, and despite all the craziness we'd just experienced, I found myself thinking *"What a beautiful area. I'd come back here again sometime."*

When we got back to the rappel base, I asked my stick partner to fill out my ICT5 task book for the fire. He said he'd feel more than comfortable signing me off as an ICT5 right then and there after that experience, but I went on to do a couple more trainee assignments anyhow. Not surprisingly, they were very tame in comparison.

Nearly thirteen years have gone by since rappelling onto the Horse Fire. For my 30th birthday, I did a ski tour of the basin where the Horse Fire had taken place. Six years ago, I hiked into that same basin with a friend while I was eight months pregnant. Five years ago, I took my daughter on her first backpacking trip to the basin and pointed out a small patch of burned trees on the ridgeline above us. Next summer, I want to take my kids, now six, and three, out there on a family backpacking trip.

Funnily enough, what started as the weirdest experience of my wildland firefighting career, has now become an integral part of our family memories and the place we call home.

Gifford Sikorsky

CUP TRENCH

Location: Leggit Fire, Idaho
Year: 2013

It's easy to take simple things for granted. Take, for example, that moment when you get a chance to take a break from your efforts and step back to admire your creation.

Although, at this particular moment, I physically lacked the ability to take a proper "step back" since I was side-stepped on an extremely steep slope (mentally calculated at over 100 percent). Still, this moment, shared collectively by our squad, was taken to admire the cup trench, which we had lovingly cut into the decaying granite on this Idaho mountainside. Adding to my sense of satisfaction was the fact that this was my very first cup trench, besides the one I'd cut into a much gentler Idaho hillside during training two months previous. As we'd learned in Fire Guard School, the humble cup trench serves a very big purpose. To catch rolling embers, logs, and other debris, and to prevent them from igniting unburned material below.

With each cup trench built, you tend to learn the secrets of success.

Dig the trench about 18"-24" across and 12" deep (actual size varies in the field). If possible, build the trench close to the object you're trying to prevent from rolling; momentum can easily overcome a cup trench. The trench should exhibit a few special features. The downhill lip of the trench should be high and strong; this is designed to stop rolling logs. Use rocks or any other nonflammable material to build this downhill lip of the trench up to the point that you're satisfied that it will be able to sufficiently catch and stop rolling materials.

As with most things in life, this is easier said than done. Use large rocks, small rocks, all rocks. All a pain in the ass.

Ideally, you'll be digging into a nice hillside with great footing and soft, rock-free soil with a slightly clay-like composition. However, I have yet to encounter such a hillside, and I doubt one exists. At least the rocks that you spend countless minutes extracting from the ground can be useful for building up the trench. There is definitely an art to cup trench construction.

The need for this particular cup trench came in the form of a large tree that had burned up and fallen over. Still smoldering, and lying haphazardly across the steep slope. We needed a cup trench to mitigate the hazard of it breaking apart and potentially sending burning fragments to start a fire below us.

By the midpoint in the process of building the cup trench, everyone had already swapped tools at least once, with each of our diverse tools having its own benefits.

My pulaski was great for breaking up weaker rocks or prying loose large ones. Tony's rhino was handy for quickly moving lots of gravel and soil. Anna's combi pick was good for getting behind large rocks to pry them out where my pulaski couldn't reach, and her combi shovel was great for moving loose material.

If you aren't familiar with these fire tools, I'd be happy to give you a quick primer.

A pulaski is what you'd get if you merged a mattock and an axe: the mattock end is good for scraping and prying but is only about four inches across. The axe end is great for chopping trees, logs, or roots.

The rhino is what you'd get if you took a garden shovel, cut the blade in half horizontally, then bent it over. Basically, a garden hoe but stronger, wider, and with a slight curve to it. It's a great scraping tool with its wider head, and okay for some limited chopping.

The combination tool, or "combi," is a military entrenching tool on a long handle. A shovel blade and a 1" wide spike can be used independently or in tandem. The shovel side is great for scraping and digging. You have two edges to choose from: a wide flat edge and then the serrated edge if you need more cutting power. The spike is good for loosening up soil and rocks, prying out rocks, and getting hard-to-reach areas.

At this point in time, I was a huge fan of the pulaski, partially due to the fact that I was a rookie; the most inexperienced on our small crew. But I did truly enjoy the capabilities a pulaski offered, even at the expense of its additional heft. I proudly carried the same pulaski with few interruptions for two seasons in Idaho but eventually replaced it with a combi for my next season in Arizona.

During the slow and exhaustive trenching process, a sort of childish glee would wash over our squad whenever someone managed to fully excavate a large rock that had been holding us up.

Loosen the rock, roll the rock, add it to the downhill lip, reinforce, keep digging. Engage in causal banter, bullshit, bond over a dirty joke, establish a friendship based on a mutual admiration of Johnny Horton, and re-assert footing. Swing, scrape, sweat, dig and hydrate.

We even had our trial by fire. A small chunk of the burning log rolled downhill while we were still in construction mode, but was successfully captured by the nearly completed cup trench.

All this took place in the span of around 30 minutes; a short time period in an otherwise long day.

As we finished our admiration break, I awkwardly maneuvered around the cup trench to begin the arduous march uphill when a shout came from the squad upslope of us. Heads turned uphill, then swiveled around behind us, as we followed their extended arms.

We heard a low roar from below, and our gazes were greeted with a column of smoke engulfing a large subalpine fir at the toe of the slope, an area that we'd just finished working in before transitioning to work on the cup trench. Brady and Anna took off downhill to deal with our mistake as the rest of us silently contemplated our error and continued uphill to meet the other squad. As I trudged upslope, the prominent thought in my mind was; *do good work, do it well, and stay alert.*

Courtney McGee

SHUTDOWN

Location: Fall Creek Fire
Year: 2008

Whenever our crew was in the field doing project work during the height of fire season, we would adhere to the daily 2 pm chainsaw shutdown requirement. The mandatory shutdown takes place because fire danger increases in the late afternoons and even a small spark has potential to start a fire.

Well, one day, after running our chainsaws all shift, we were just about to pack up for the day when we got dispatched to a new fire start. Responding to that fire turned our regular eight hour shift into a delirious 32-hour stretch.

At some point, while we were working away in the wee hours of the night one of our rookie swampers shouted out, *"We missed our 2 o'clock shutdown for saws!"*

Huge bouts of laughter could be heard up and down the fireline as people continued to rebelliously rev their chainsaws under the cover of darkness. That comment managed to live on for the rest of the season, becoming yet another inside joke on our crew.

Bre Orcasitas

THE ROOKIE VAN

Location: Redmond, Oregon
Year: 2010

Smokejumper rookie training is a five-week long stretch of having absolutely no idea what is going to happen next... all day, every day. The trainers pride themselves on keeping rookies in a constant state of anxiousness while also pushing you to the very edge of your physical and mental capacity. Us rookies were feeling these sentiments to the core, when one day, the trainers yelled for us to all pile into the 15-passenger van that we'd grown so accustomed to. With the anxiousness and dread looming heavy as we scurried toward the van, obeying every command as usual, one of my fellow rookies blurted out in a sweet and sincere voice, *"are you taking us to the pancake house down the street??"*

It was a tiny shining moment of hilarity that gave all us rookies a good laugh before the next onslaught of physical

and mental challenges that awaited us on the other side
of the van ride.

WATCH THIS

Location: Farnham Fire, California
Year: 1992

The twenty of us had been up for about 40 hours or so. We had all shown up to work the previous morning and did our PT before setting out to do some project work; thinning and building hand piles. Then, in the afternoon we got dispatched to a new start where we dug fireline all day, into the night, through to the next morning, and into the afternoon again.

Most of us knew how to pace ourselves on a long shift; keep moving, chase spots. Do a little burning to speed up line construction, think about safety. Don't ponder about how much longer it'll be until we'll get a break, keep moving. Then finally, we got word that another crew had shown up on the incident to replace us so we hiked back to the rigs, stowing our saws and tools in the bins without a refurb —a real sharpening would have to wait. As you might imagine, we were spent.

As we started to head out, our supt. (superintendent) informed us over the tac channel that the road was blocked up ahead by a piece of broken-down equipment. Not to worry though, there was another way out, just not as direct. And so, down a dirt road we went. The supt. truck went first, then the two crew buggies. We drove for a while; turning here, and turning there. Then after a while, things began to seem familiar.

Did we already go by that tree? Are we driving in circles?!

We drove on, still following the supt. I was riding in the second buggy; which was the third and last vehicle in our tired and ridiculous parade. The captain on our buggy saw an intersection where the other two rigs went straight.

He told our driver, "Turn right, that's the way out of here. I'm tired of following these guys and driving around in circles."

He grabbed the mic to let them know which way we'd gone, and eventually, all the rigs arrived at the fairgrounds where we would get some much-needed sleep.

In the world of firefighting there's already a fair amount of "lining out," but our high-strung, very "Type A" supt. took it to a whole new level. His plan was to go and scout for a suitable sleeping area, but instead of letting the crew kick it in the vehicles, he had us line out in tool order with our red bags while he did his scouting. Some people stood in line with their red bags on the ground next to them while others held onto theirs by putting an arm through one strap. Our exhausted crew had nothing to do but stand there and wait; hopelessly staring off into space.

I was toward the back of the line standing next to my roommate thinking this would never end, when all of a sudden, he turned to me and said "Watch this."

So, I watched as he glanced at the guy in front of him, then I noticed how he positioned himself in just such a way. Before my mind could put two and two together, he picked up his red bag and quickly slung it over his shoulder, which smacked into the guy in front of him. That guy lost his balance, and lunged forward, tripping over his own red bag and knocking into the person in front of him, and on it went, just like dominos!

Just as the supt. was coming back from his scouting mission, he caught the spectacle of a few people in line falling and tripping all over themselves and yelled out, "What the FUCK are you guys doing?!!!"

I truly don't know how I didn't pee my pants.

It's hard to say if the supt. learned a lesson or not, but after the domino incident, he never had us line out while he looked for a sleeping area again. The lesson I learned that night was that if my roommate ever said "Watch this" I was going to watch.

Kate Averett

THE DIGS

With fingers firmly grasped
Upon the sleek wooden grain
Their grip tightens.
Swing after swing,
They carve into the arid earth
Quietly washing the dirt wake aside.

Sodden with sweat
The desert glistens.
But, cracks protrude,
Funneling the drops
Of lustrous heroism
Through canyons of age.

Worn well, but weary
The hours of grit and grime
Remain nameless.

With only one record kept
On a single organ
playing a constant tune.

CHAPTER 3

Lasting Moment

The best fire is the one you're on.

Logbook for the PT hike of fire crews and local community members. Entiat, WA.

Ian Morgan

DIVISION WAKE UP

Location: B&B Complex, Central Oregon
Year: 2003

As I think back to my first year as a hotshot there are many stories worth telling, but one stands out above all the rest. It's funny how some stories become legendary, living on to be told, and retold. I'd attribute this to two factors; story significance, and the characters themselves. A good story can live on for years or generations within a crew and even meander to different crews, continuing the network of tradition and story.

My story begins near the end of the fire season in Central Oregon on the B and B complex in 2003. The fire itself spanned over the Cascade Mountain range, and was being managed by two different IMTs; one on either side of the mountains. This led to all sorts of interesting decisions being made, one of which, was to issue every single firefighter a photo ID; a decision that, to this day, still remains a mystery to me. As you might imagine, the photo collection process was extremely inefficient and left impatient firefighters waiting in yet another long line.

Being that it was September, our crew had lost a couple of folks who were headed back to school, at least until they graduated college and decided to make a career out of firefighting. This meant that our crew would have a need for fill-ins , and for some reason, which I still can't figure out, the superintendent was willing to take my recommendation.

My recommendation was this guy Bobby, whom I'd met while working the year before on a Type ll regular crew from Western Washington. Bobby and I had formed a friendship founded on our interest in labor and what I'd like to believe was a high level of intellectual commonality, but it was more likely a bond of shared suffering.

Anybody in fire could tell you that integrating with a hotshot crew in early September is not an easy task. This phenomenon was something I actually paid close attention to throughout my years as a hotshot because fill-ins who join up in late fire season can break quickly if they aren't hearty or fire-hardened in some capacity. That's because by then, the crew is extremely fire fit and operating very smoothly together. I wasn't concerned for Bobby though. He hailed from Southeastern Alaska and was more in tune with being in the woods than most. He was the type of person who took pride in his pulaski being sharp and was always ready for work. Bobby took to the group quickly, not taking any gruff and keeping the air light.

Our division consisted of another hotshot crew and a type ll crew assigned to the same task of cold-trailing the edge of the fire. We were all spiked out near a boy scout camp that was also being protected during the fire's more active periods. At our spike camp we had room to set up tents or rack out with enough space for privacy, but within a reasonable distance, in case the crew needed to be woken up and accounted for quickly. Bobby chose to set up camp a little bit away from the rest of the crew so he wouldn't disturb others since he had a tendency to talk in his sleep and move around. I could relate, as I had a tendency to do the same.

Unfortunately, the weather began to get more damp. So much so, that the predicted overnight rain drove all three crews to move inside one of the boy scout camp buildings, which was essentially one large room that seemed to be utilized as the eating lodge or large gathering space. The A-frame building had hardwood floors and a large triangular floor-to-ceiling window at one end of the building.

Sixty-plus firefighters claimed their space on the floor,

more or less, side by side as space became a premium, but everyone was happy to be out of the rain. As firefighters went to bed many read books or played cards before calling it a night. Most of us were exhausted from a long, hard season and tough shifts. This type of cumulative exhaustion can make for wonderful sleep; dead-to-the-world type sleep.

That level of exhaustion, and hard sleep shared by all, probably had a hand in making what happened next so disorienting. I have no concept of what time it was, all I know is that everyone in the building had just been woken up in unison by a blood-curdling scream. A scream that, just by hearing it, made other tired and confused firefighters begin screaming too. Now, there were sixty firefighters who'd just been startled awake from a dead sleep, trying to figure out what was happening; myself being one of them.

As I frantically looked around our lead digger grabbed my attention. He was sitting up in his sleeping bag, and he appeared to be rowing backward across the gym.

He was screaming, "Stop! Help! Getaway!"

In all the confusion it took me a minute to realize that beyond the strange antics of our lead digger, it was actually Bobby who was the main concern. Still, in a sleep state, he had leaped out of his sleeping bag, screaming and running through the lodge at full sprint, leaping over tables, and dodging between sixty freaked-out firefighters who were all sandwiched into a small space. He was running straight toward the large window at the end of the building.

One of the squad leaders from our crew tried to position himself to tackle the sleeping assailant, while another crewmember who'd already had experience with night terrors like these muttered, "Here we go again."

Fortunately, someone from one of the other crews managed to shine a light directly in Bobby's face, which effectively woke him from his night terror. Now awake, but pretty disoriented, Bobby muttered to the crew foreman, "Are we cool?" to which the foreman replied, "Fuck no! We are NOT cool."

The next day after all the chaos had died down and people had gotten some sleep, Bobby explained how he had been dreaming that he was running from an avalanche. He told us he was headed toward the window with the intention of jumping through it to escape. This made me realize that as crazy as that night was, it could've actually been worse! That wild night was the only one we spent inside the boy scout building; after that, the weather cleared enough for us to move back outside to the safety of our own personal space.

As I reflect back on this story it prompted me to look for pictures from that fire. I found photos of the boy scout camp, and the daily work with lots of smiles throughout, which I was glad to see because that is the way I remembered it. Many of the people in those photos have moved on to other work. Two of them are airline pilots, and three are structure firefighters. Then there's a city planner, a UPS driver, a personal trainer, and a teacher. Of course, many of them stayed in wildfire too, moving into fire management, and regional jobs, filling out their years until finding themselves eligible for retirement.

That division wake-up was one for the record books, and I can say with absolute certainty that no one sleeping in that room will ever forget that night. Whenever I run into any of the fellow firefighters who I shared that experience with, this story always comes up, as everyone takes turns retelling their version of the mayhem.

Bobby stayed with the crew for a second roll, but that was the last the crew saw of him. Now, however, you may find yourself being whisked across the Pacific Ocean with Bobby as your pilot aboard one of the major US airlines.

Jess Westbrook

OUT WITH A BOO!

Location: New Mexico
Year: 2019

In the summer of 2019, I traveled from the Wayne National Forest in Ohio to join up with an IA crew from Region 3 in order to work on my FFT1 task book. Not long after I arrived, we mobilized, bouncing around to a few different areas. On one of the slow days, we found a good place to park where we could hang out, and also look out over the surrounding area.

Another crewmember and I decided to walk along a nearby dirt path that cut through a grass field; the grass easily towering above our heads. We were sharing a bag of cherries as we strolled along when all of a sudden, the crew boss came barreling out of the tall grass, very effectively (and very intentionally) scaring the shit out of us! I was so startled that I leapt off my feet, sending cherries flying in every direction while my fellow crewmember nearly fell over. He got us good.

I looked at him and said, "You just wait. I'll get you back."
And I left it at that.

The summer continued on, and I stayed with the crew
until September before it was time to head back to Ohio.
We were assigned to a fire on the Mt. Taylor District of the
Cibola National Forest for my last night with the crew. The
next day I'd be on the line for half a day, then have to head
into town and catch my flight home. Of course, I had one
final task before leaving. I needed to get the crew boss
back before hopping on that plane for home.

The fire camp was a small one, set up by the local forest
staff. Our vehicles were on the opposite side of the dirt
road from camp. The area where we had parked wasn't lit
up at night, so most folks used headlamps or phone flash-
lights to make their way back in the dark. A few of the girls
and I were done with dinner first, so we went back to the
trucks to wait for the rest of the crew before driving further
up the road to our sleeping spot.

I told them, "Watch this," as I nestled myself into the floor-
board of the crew boss' truck, getting ready to exact my
revenge.

I was probably there, in total darkness, for about ten minutes before I heard someone approaching. I was really

hoping that it was the crew boss, rather than the crew boss trainee... either way, someone was about to have the surprise of their life.

As the door opened, I sprang up from the floorboards with a holler and was greeted with a terrified yell from the crew boss and a cell phone to the face! Almost the entire crew was there to witness the show and to get a good laugh, the crew boss included. *Got 'em.*

Sy Holmes

THE THINGS WE HAULED AROUND IN THE BUS

Location: Alaska
Year: 2022

In the beginning, there was Alaska and there was the pile. It wasn't a small pile, or even a medium-sized pile, but a large pile. It included the crucial earthly belongings of 20 people. Enough water and MREs to last us five days; tarps, chainsaws, pulaskis, shovels, fuel for the chainsaws, drip torches, fuel for the drip torches, a massive container of Folger's coffee, a couple of pots and pans, silverware, several gallons of military-grade insect repellent that might have rendered us all sterile, and some random knick-knacks that they told us would be useful in the "Last Frontier" but never were. These were the things we hauled in and out of a decommissioned Fairbanks Borough school bus. We kept a tally on Maddie's notepad of all the times we moved the pile and would holler out whenever she added another tick mark.

When we left Fort Wainwright, they told us we would be at our final destination soon. They told us we needed to be ready to get on a boat, then a plane, then a helicopter. So, we were. We moved, split, and reconfigured the pile. Then they told us to get back on the bus. Somewhere outside of Fairbanks, there was a fire, but we had made big, elegant loops around the city several times and hadn't seen one. Inside the bus, it smelled like swamp ass and DEET. The Alaskan interior, if you haven't been there, is just Florida if Florida was frozen two-thirds of the year and had bears instead of gators. Everything else is basically the same.

"Damn, bro," Stav said as we leaned on each other in the bench seat, "where are we even going?"

I didn't know. We were going wherever the universe needed us to go, I suppose. The ways of the Alaska fire service, like those of God, are inscrutable. The midnight sun hung above us constantly and I wasn't going to sleep anyway, so I just mixed some more instant coffee in my Nalgene and settled in. Then rumors began moving through the crew. People thought we were getting reassigned up above the Arctic Circle, or that they might send us back home. Obviously, the federal government for whom we worked, had officially declared us all losers who deserved to stay on the bus forever. I became spiritual on the bus. I texted my friend Lindsey my exact birth time so she could consult the star charts. I learned that everything was going to get better. I learned that things were unclear. I learned that the Magic 8-Ball is a surprisingly accurate tool for forecasting the future when you work for the feds.

The bus wasn't without its charms. Our driver was a middle-aged German lady, Ulrike, who was recovering from a heart attack and would relentlessly hit on Jeff when he tried to speak German. At times we would see other crews stuck on their own buses, and we'd wave to them. When we stopped, we'd usually end up with another Montana hotshot crew who wandered around smoking cigarettes, feeling just as lost as us. Sometimes, when we were out of the bus, it rained and we would have to quickly tarp our pile. Sometimes our superintendent would whisper to the bus driver and we would all pile out to take a piss. Sometimes we'd just sit. Sometimes we would stop at Fred Meyer and I'd buy myself a new jumbo pack of Twizzlers.

The bus actually didn't bother me all that much. I come from small-town North Carolina where waiting for things that probably aren't going to happen is the American pastime, baseball be damned. The ability to stare slack-jawed into the middle distance for long stretches of time has propelled my friends and me to minor success, or at least it's kept us from getting fired in our chosen professions. It turns out that in agriculture, emergency services, the military, or any job where you have to act like you're paying attention to PowerPoint presentations, it's a good skill set to have. It makes a lot of people without redneck Jedi training antsy, though. There was the feeling that our time could be better spent. It could've, of course, but it just doesn't work that way. You don't get days of your life back, and on an organizational level, they're fairly cheap. In life, love, and fire, your time is going to get wasted; It's just unavoidable. You can be mad about it, or you can accept it.

Too confused to be mad, we all learned to accept it. We stood in parking lots, playgrounds, lodges at ski hills; pretty much anywhere you can stand. We would unload our pile, count it, stack it, and then get ready to reload it. Quality of life declined and nicotine consumption skyrocketed. We started sport-eating MREs. I ran out of Twizzlers. The mosquitoes ate well. With all of us sitting in front of the beat-up bus, I started to become convinced that we were part of some demented parody of "Into the Wild." The Twizzlers, MREs, and bug spray all congealed into a blob in my veins effectively cutting off blood flow to my brain. We all began to accept that this was our life now. Nothing but the bus, the pile, the mosquitos, and the occasional Alaskan rainstorm.

Bus-purgatory went on for about five days. Disoriented by the sun and the cumulative effect of a million mosquito bites, I had lost track. Our bus trip finally ended on a long-grade coming down from an Air Force radar station that we had been stuck at for some reason. As we glided down, the rear wheels started screeching with the unmistakable sound of metal-on-metal. It's the kind of sound you hear when something crucial has failed. Next to me, my squad leader closed his eyes and let out a low, long groan. I gave a nod to the "Big Man" if this was, in fact, it. Ulrike pulled to the side of the road and it took a few hundred yards for us to stop. From behind us, the other crew flew by on their bus with one of their wheel wells on fire. We ran up with a fire extinguisher and put it out. They all piled off their bus, smoked a quick cigarette, then got back on and kept going as we sat and waited for our school bus's owner to show up.

After a couple of hours, the owner arrived. He figured the bus was probably fine, but said he'd drive it just to make sure. We thought maybe that meant he would take it on a test lap to see if the brakes were still there. We were wrong. It turned out what he meant was that he would drive it but our asses would all still be riding on it. We didn't have anything better to do, so we agreed. And anyways, the pile was still on it and we didn't feel like pulling it all off again. So, we hopped back on as the owner announced that he was taking us back into town.

"You guys wanna see a musk ox?" he asked, "it'll only be about a 30-minute detour."

Yeah man, sure, we got no place else to be.

The brakes didn't give out. The musk ox was impressive. It was all good. We ended up back where we started.

Bre Orcasitas

SUBSTANDARD HOUSE GUEST

Location: Wyoming
Year: 2012

It's funny how the memory fades over time in some respects, yet remains completely intact in others. I can't remember the exact month, but it was hot, supremely hot, actually. The year was 2012, which was yet another fire season on the hotshot crew for me. Our crew had been bouncing around between fires in South Dakota, and Wyoming during a 14-day assignment that ultimately turned into back-to-back fire assignments.

It was sometime within this excessively long roll that we found ourselves working an IA fire that completely worked us over. After what felt like an endless shift, the crew decided to bed down and start fresh in the morning.

A pretty standard sleeping practice on the fireline is to

simply lay a space blanket down, roll out your sleeping pad and sleeping bag over top, and call it a night. A tent can be nice when there's a concern about adverse weather, but on a clear night it amounts to ten minutes of unnecessary effort. This happened to be a clear night so I cozied up in my sleeping bag and rolled onto my side, easily falling asleep with an assist from pure exhaustion.

It was somewhere in the middle of the night when I awoke to an odd sensation. I felt something heavy pushing on me as I lay on my side. Being that I was half asleep I didn't think about what it could be, I just gave a strong "STOP PUSHING ON ME" shrug with my arm against the weight. The next thing I felt was a firm, deep grip on my upper arm and a brief -but heavy- weight pushing even harder on me before it was completely lifted. It was right at that moment when I heard the very distinct sound of a large bird of prey flapping its wings as it took flight. Now fully awake, I came to realize that an owl had just landed on me! I could sense its dissatisfaction with using me as a perch by the aggressive force in which its talons gripped me before taking its leave.

After that surreal and sobering experience, I spent some quality time staring up at the stars pondering just how immersed in the natural environment fire folks actually are. Sleeping on the ground night after night isn't out of the ordinary, in fact, that is the ordinary. Several months a year -every year- are spent almost entirely outside in the elements. Those who live this life can attest that nothing could ever feel more truly in line with human nature than being among nature itself. That knowing seems to transcend words, but is easily felt. The forest becomes your living room, your easy chair; your bedroom. But it's not yours alone; and every so often our animal friends let us know we're merely guests in their home.

Sara Sweeney

NIGHT SHIFT IN WILLOW CREEK, CA

Location: Willow Creek, California
Year: 2021

I.

These night shifts always mess with me a little at first, even though there is some weird cachet to working all night and making it through as if you have survived something. But night is not made for going direct... it's made for burning off miles of roads and dozer lines and then holding it all. Going direct in the darkness is, in most cases, just tempting fate.

So, then we wait. We drink coffee and build warming fires, and talk idly about nothing much important—or everything important. These are the kind of conversations that, at 0200, you have over either strong coffee or bad whiskey... and we don't have any whiskey.

ll.

One of the perks to doing this job that outlasts all of the agonies is that you get to meet and work with some of the last true originals. You get to operate with people who are honest, and hard, and raw, the kind you don't find in very many places anymore. This job harbors a few—it's one of the last professions that are still friendly to people who work hard and want to, who tell the truth and live by it, who understand the value of honesty and labor.

These are the people I want to surround myself with in this world.

Will Silverman

FIRE FLOE

Watching the world burn
From a 737
While a foreground
Of August ice glistens
Ignites a new level
Of understanding

The Gulf of Alaska
An unforgiving landscape
Of barren islands
Silted straits
Glaciers calving
And masked moraines
Embossed by Satan's
Breath leaves only one
Conclusion about Earth's condition

Who brought this wrath
Upon her? Who sparked
The last goodbye

To this living legend
Sharp in contrast
To the one that
Brought us life?

ART

When in doubt, add a swivel.

More Fire on the Landscape by: Chris Hensley

Helicopter by: Chase Burgett

Engine 414 by: Marisa Duarte

Bull Elk by: Sheena Waters

Bridger-Teton by: Sheena Waters

'Booker' by: Leona Allen

CHAPTER 4
That's How It Goes

Ounces make pounds.

Logbook for the PT hike of fire crews and local community members. Entiat, WA.

Courtney McGee

NAKED PEOPLE

Location: Terwilliger Fire
Year: 2018

A report about a smoldering stump at a popular hot spring on our local district had been called in. The first person on scene let dispatch know about the chaos that was ensuing by relaying over the radio for all to hear; *"There are naked people frantically running down the trail!"*

Forest E. Ployer

FIRST FIRE

Location: Ash Fire, Arizona
Year: 1999

It was 0530, and you could hear the rumble in the barracks. "GET UP! FIRE CALL. GET UP!"

It was my very first wildland fire since being on the crew, cool! A fly's buzzing could have woken me that night, as I lay there in anticipation. My bunkmate was less enthusiastic.

Throwing his feet over the top bunk, he told me, "We ain't no heroes kid, keep that in mind, and you'll be all right."

We gathered our gear and moved toward the gate to get on the bus. Excitement still filled me as I heard the crew boss yelling to ensure we had everything loaded and secure, then he counted us as we got on the twelve-seat, four-wheel drive bus. As we pulled out, we were told that the fire was on the Coconino National Forest about an acre in size, and called the Ash fire, ETA- one hour.

I spent the entire ride looking out the window, examining every dust cloud, asking myself, "is that it?" Then I noticed something different. A single gray and white column off in the distance, not much taller than the tree line. *Is that it?*

The crew boss yelled down the aisle, "We'll be at the staging area in ten!"

That *is* it! I could barely contain all my excitement.

The staging area was actually just a pull-off along the road where we met the IC. We received orders to work the west flank of the fire with a type III engine from the local district and spent the next eight hours mopping up the fire. I had never worked so hard, or gotten so dirty working in my life, but something in me enjoyed the work.

At 1700, the crew boss told us to head back to the bus so we could return to the barracks. *What a great day!* As we loaded up, I spotted a single sign at the end of the pull-out that must have been placed there while we were working.

It simply stated in colorfully written text, " Thank you, heroes!"

The ride back was calm, and even as the gates of the Winslow Prison welcomed us back once again, I thought to myself, *"I guess he was wrong. We are heroes."*

Brent Ruby

HAUNTED BY SAMPLES

Location: Montana
Year: 1997

Tucked away in the back of a ranger station, I followed the ticking of a metronome, which guided my stepping cadence, up-up, down-down. Unfortunately, my stomach was filled to the brim with a hearty helping of turkey and gravy, dramatically influencing my heart rate during this otherwise modest exercise feat. I was beginning to realize that my opportunity for scientific data collection from the nearby hotshot crew was about to be thwarted by my insatiable, and ill-timed appetite for gravy.

Upon arrival in Lincoln, Montana my research team (which consisted of myself, and a graduate student) met up with the local hotshot crew to enroll a few of their crewmembers into our initial research project. However, the chosen meet-up location was Lambkin's diner, which was home to the previously mentioned irresistible gravy that all but doomed me to failure in the fitness capacity step test.

Not more than a year prior, I had submitted a research grant to the US Army to study the total energy demands of wildland fire management and suppression. The goal was to employ a gold standard research methodology involving oral delivery of two stable isotopes (^{2}H and ^{18}O in an expensive cocktail called the doubly labeled water method) by using hotshots on varied assignments as the test subjects.

While this technique had been used during military training exercises, there was something attractive to the Army about studying unscripted wildland fire operations. It was an opportunity to use a laboratory/clinical technique in the field and a wildfire near Lincoln was our first opportunity to deploy. However, the local district would only allow us access to the fire camp if we held a red card certification and the associated fitness test quals.

The thing is, we were showing up after the required 'Standards for Survival' mandatory pre-season training. At that time (July of 1997), the standard hiring requirement also included the step test, or a timed 1 ½ mile run as an alternative.

The metronome was shut off and I sat down to wait for the pulse count to be recorded, which would be used in combination with my body weight, and age to estimate my aerobic capacity. I failed miserably; denied by gravy. I quickly requested that we be allowed to perform the alternative 1 ½ mile run (required finish time of 11:40). Eyebrows were raised but they allowed it. My graduate student and I finished well below the required time limit, albeit uncomfortably so, due to full stomachs. The admission ticket to my first fire camp was granted, and we arranged a meet-up later that night with the hotshot crew to initiate our study.

Since 1997 we've used doubly labeled water in several studies in unique field settings, but this was our debut. The scary part about the process is that each research subject consumes what amounts to about six ounces of labeled water with a price tag of around a thousand dollars. The method required what we figured to be about 5-7 days of work on a fire to allow the calculations. We decided to start the study conservatively and only provide the doses to one male, and one female. The two hotshots consumed the carefully prepared dose vials of labeled water by light of headlamp while their fellow crewmembers crowded around to provide a healthy dose of laughter about the impending nude body weight, and urine collections that would take place for the two subjects over the next several days.

The small fire near Lincoln petered out within a couple of days, so the hotshot crew was reassigned to the Hopper fire on the Los Padres National Forest. Buying last-minute plane tickets and heading to California to chase down costly urine samples felt like being called up to "The Show."

We were headed for the big time, *or so it felt.* We got our mobile research lab set up (consisting of a 2-person pup tent and a cooler) and waited for the crew to return to fire camp at the end of their first shift. It was about 9:00 PM (*sorry,* 2100) when the crew wandered back into camp after being shuttled by helicopter from the main fire. We collected our urine samples and dosed three more hotshots. I was on cloud nine of urine sample heaven, and I realized that unique science was possible outside the confines of a traditional laboratory setting.

Damn it, I was wearing Whites (that were minimally broken in), a borrowed yellow shirt, and Nomex pants, which housed my very first red card; I felt like a rogue scientist, and I liked it! And to cap things off, the hotshot crew enjoyed having us around. Maybe they were just humoring me, or maybe they saw us as some weird-ass version of a science-focused pair of groupies; regardless, it felt pretty great.

Eventually, the time came for us to finish the study on one of the firefighters we started with in Lincoln. We planned to see the crew at the end of their shift back in camp, however, the shift plan... shifted. Now the crew would be staying out on the line, coyote style. The incident management team was incredibly accommodating toward our effort and organized a helicopter flight so that we could capture our final urine sample and measure of body weight. The feeling of badass scientist ratcheted up to an 11 as we landed at a drop point along the fire's edge. We connected with the crew in the early evening, still feeling quite excited about our coyote science adventure.

Collecting a urine sample in the wilderness is relatively easy. *Have the person pee in a cup, then transfer it to test tubes for storage.* However, a measure of nude body weight on a two-thousand-dollar digital scale was more of a challenge. We leveled the scale on a flat rock surface, then held up a tarp between our guy and the rest of the crew. If smartphones would have been a thing back then I'm certain someone would have cued up some Barry White!

We closed up the study with the rest of our research subjects a few days later in fire camp, trying our best to act as if we actually knew what we were doing. Then, before we knew it, we had boarded a plane headed for Spokane, Washington only to jump in a car for a three-hour-long, late-night drive to Missoula.

No matter, I had my cooler of seemingly priceless urine samples, and was feeling pretty happy about our success-ful trip. I hit the pillow in Missoula around 1:30 AM (*sorry, 0130*) trying my best not to wake my two year-old daugh-ter and sleeping wife. My mind wandered for a short while about fire boot blisters, helicopter rides, fire camp food, and the unique smell of urine samples in the morning at a coyote camp. But then sleep came. Early the next morning I was awoken by my wife poking me with what felt like a popsicle stick. Fighting through the blurred, sleepy vision I tried to get my eyes into focus. It was then that my wife said, "I wanted to wait to pee on the stick until you got home from California, DADDY." Nine months later our son was born.

Later that summer I was thrilled to hear from one of the hotshot crew's test subjects who was calling to invite me to their end-of-the-year party.

"Really?! I'll be there!" My response was an enthusiastic yes, but to be clear, the invite was more rhetorical than an

actual question. If I was invited, they expected me to show up.

It was interesting to see everybody -mostly cleaned up- and in full-on party mode as the beer and stories flowed freely throughout the night; I was beginning to feel like I was genuinely part of the crew.

Then one of the crewmembers approached me and said, "Ruby. Time for a game of pool. You're my partner. You break."

I chalked up a cue and refamiliarized myself with the landscape of a pool table. While I may have played here or there growing up (mostly at summer camps), I was by no means, a pool shark. I sunk one ball and positioned for another shot, which also went in. After the third shot was successful, the crew began to take notice. When balls 4, 5, and 6 dropped in, the back area of the bar grew quiet. I sunk ball number 7 and the quiet turned to pin-drop silence. I slowly walked the perimeter of the table, called the pocket, and sunk the eight ball. The room erupted as I completed perhaps the greatest athletic feat of my life in front of this entire crew of badasses. The rest of the evening was a blur.

It's been more than 25 years since those urine samples

were collected, and that epic game of 8-ball took place, but I still keep in contact with some of the crew that I had the pleasure to work with early on. I've shared laughs, hugs, and tears with that initial hotshot crew, and many others over the years.

Since we first began, our research team has published several papers specific to wildland firefighters and we continue to work with crews. I sometimes feel like a research missionary, a Johnny Appleseed character of sorts, dedicated to sharing our science in order to improve the health, safety, and performance of the wildland firefighting community.

I have certainly learned that genuine mayhem, unpredictability, and hilarity unfold when you stomp out of the lab in fire boots and refuse to turn back.

In the novel, *A River Runs Through It,* writer, professor, and fisherman Norman Maclean ends the book with a simple statement; "I am haunted by waters."

I can relate as a writer, professor, part-time fisherman, and researcher.

Except, *"I am haunted by samples."*

Bre Orcasitas

THE FIREFIGHTER IN THE MEADOW

Location: Washington
Year: 2012

Armageddon. It's a phrase we use when there's a significant lightning bust that produced far more new starts than there are firefighters to staff them. This time Armageddon took place on my home forest in Washington; the Okanogan-Wenatchee.

The morning after the lightning bust, fire resources were being dispatched the way a toddler plays 52 pick up. You start out with all the cards in your hand, then fling them in every direction in a moment of excited panic, and before you know it, they're all gone.

I can't remember which load I was on that day, but nevertheless, I do recall lifting off in the helicopter from the rappel base headed for the coordinates of the fire we'd been requested to. Our time enroute was about 20 minutes, and those 20 minutes provided some of the wildest visuals of my fire career.

Up until then, the term Armageddon had always been a joke, but that flight led me to think that maybe perhaps the end was indeed upon us! There were columns of smoke rising in every direction with a more distinct smokey haze collectively blanketing the earth; the smell of it penetrating the aircraft all the while.

Eventually, we arrived at the coordinates. The spotter had his work cut out for him that day, sizing up fires from the air and turning down one new start after the next due to the high levels of risk associated with each. Because fires were quite literally everywhere, it was difficult to staff a new start that didn't have another one below it, etc. Finally, the spotter and all rappellers onboard agreed upon a new start that wouldn't place us in a compromising position. In order to staff the fire, we first needed to make positive contact with dispatch over the radio, *seems simple enough.* Turns out, *not so simple.* The frequencies were all jammed up with excessive radio traffic forest wide and after many, many, attempts the spotter proved to be unsuccessful. Since we were now running low on fuel from burning circles in the sky to size up fires, the decision was made to head back to the rappel base.

Fortunately, the dispatch center is located at the far end of the rappel base so once we landed the spotter marched over to make positive contact the old-fashioned way. In the meantime, I sprinted to the bathroom, desperately trying to unhook my rappel harness and shimmy out of my flight suit before peeing my pants. Once the helicopter had been refueled, we hopped in again and made our way back to the fire.

As it turned out, there happened to be a picture-perfect landing spot near the fire, so we opted to land rather than rappel. By the time we finally hit the ground, configured our gear, and had a second load of rappellers dropped, it was nearing dusk so we high-tailed it over to the fire for a good look around before nightfall. When I say we high-tailed it, I mean it. I'm pretty sure every inch of ground between the meadow and the fire's edge was taken up by jackstraw dead-and-down trees, which had us flopping over top of them like a bunch of drunken hurdlers. After a bit of fiddling around on the fire we hurdled our way back to the meadow for the night, which would act as our base camp and safety zone for the rest of our time on incident #588.

The next day we had won the 'fire resources' lottery and had been allotted two dozers, two type 6 engines, and a handcrew; not to mention some air resources to provide water drops as available. I spent a good chunk of the shift with another rappeller building a p-line between the fire's edge and the meadow so that we could actually have an obstruction free escape route to our safety zone. By the end of the day, it seemed that we had all but knocked the fire out; our only real challenge of the shift having been sketchy radio communications.

Later, back at camp we were all feeling pretty confident we'd be able to hand off the fire by the end of the next shift. After patching together dinners from our food boxes and having a few laughs I drifted off to sleep thinking how nice it was that night; at least 10 degrees warmer than the night before.

In the morning, we popped up from our sleeping bags like gophers, wiping the sleep from our eyes while sipping on instant coffee and munching on the rappel world's much beloved Mountain House Blueberry and Granola breakfast meals. I'd say our collective morning mood was, casual. Then one of us noticed a small plume of smoke in the general vicinity of our fire. Funnily enough, because there were so many fires in the area, we couldn't be certain that the smoke was actually coming from our fire or one nearby without hiking over to confirm it. After sending a runner over to have a look, and getting verification over the radio, the mood became much less casual. We had a spot fire to deal with, and not only that, it was burning quite well in the jackstraw dead-and-down first thing in the morning. That's never a good sign. It prompted me to think back to the higher overnight temps I'd noticed before drifting off to sleep; overnight recovery? *Not so much.*

Off we dashed down the p-line to get a good look at what we were dealing with. It didn't take long to determine that we weren't going to be able to put it out; it was burning too hot. We were in sub-alpine fir, which is basically the spot fire's best friend with its magical ability to fling fire across well-established lines; so that didn't help either.

Most of the morning's events have faded in my memory. However, one thing I remember pretty clearly was that in all the chaos some random dude came driving up the dozer line in a small SUV. Dumbfounded, the IC and I stopped our conversation mid-sentence and watched as he got out of the rig and looked around in wide-eyed amazement as if he was on a sight-seeing tour. That's about when he noticed us and our expressions, which surely prompted this "sightseer" to state his purpose.

He quickly explained that he had come from fire camp because major radio frequency changes had been made to the commo plan (Since our small fire was part of a greater "fire complex" we had to use this commo plan rather than the local channels), meaning we wouldn't be able to speak to aircraft or use command, etc., without them.

Apparently, he had driven out to our fire because commo was already so bad that it was difficult to effectively communicate. The best part was that after explaining his purpose he reached into the backseat and pulled out a large 3-ring-binder along with a radio cloning cable. He told us that he was supposed to clone everyone's radios but didn't know how, so they sent him with instructions.

There he stood before us; this poor runner from fire camp with panic in his eyes, waiting for a response. We took the new frequency list and cloning cable and told him we'd deal with it. With a look of pure relief, he jumped back into his little SUV and disappeared from our lives.

After reprogramming my radio with the needed frequencies, I essentially played the firefighter version of Marco-Polo all across the fire in order to get each radio cloned. At some point, our additional resources arrived, but I can't say exactly what they were, beyond knowing that a dozer showed up, and that a couple of aircraft were working overhead dumping water on the ever-growing spot fire.

After the Marco-Polo radio clone adventure I turned into

the makeshift dozer boss, scouting and flagging a line around the spot fire for the dozer operator. Unfortunately, the sub-alpine fir struck again, flinging spot fires further ahead of itself, including on the other side of the dozer's flag line. He attempted to reroute a couple of times before we all agreed the line needed to be more indirect if we had any hope of it holding.

Like a lightbulb overhead, the p-line came to mind. It was already flagged, and was a great cut off point with the meadow being a solid anchor at the other end. The IC was onboard, so I took off down the p-line to make sure that it hadn't been compromised. Once I reached the meadow and gave the green light to the dozer, the IC asked that I button up our gear incase additional resources were to be dropped off via helicopter in the meadow/safety zone/helispot.

I had a great vantage point to see the fire activity from the meadow so I kept providing updates to the IC as I was stowing gear and in seemingly no time at all, the fire intensified to a point where I thought, *"hmmm... maybe I should shuttle this gear away from the tree line and into the meadow just in case..."*

Fortunately, the meadow was a bit larger than the size of a football field made up of about 90% dirt with a few clumps of sagebrush. It was pretty bombproof, hence, being designated as our safety zone. Somewhere in all the mayhem the dozer had been called off of the attempt to build fireline toward the meadow due to the fire's intensity, and eventually, the IC ordered all resources to disengage from the fire and go to safety.

This is where things got interesting. I had no idea where everyone else was. The fire was pushing in the direction of the meadow so they couldn't get to the safety zone. It was just me and eight rappeller's worth of gear all by my lonesome. All the other rappellers knew my location and that I was safe, and I got confirmation that they were safe as well (even though I had no idea where they ended up), so we moved on to the next order of business; my extraction.

The plan was for our crew's helicopter (which had been doing water drops) to return to the base, unhook the long-line and bucket, and grab an additional person before returning to pick me up. We thought it best to have an additional person along to help load all the gear. Plan B being, I'd have to wait out the fire burning around me in the meadow before getting a ride. Since I had eight rappeller's worth of food boxes and more water than I could possibly drink, I felt pretty good about the potential of hanging out to watch the big show. *Well, here's to the best laid plans.*

At some point in my continuous saga of hoisting and lugging rappel gear and cargo further, and further into the meadow while scanning a billion channels on the radio at once, I heard some attention-grabbing commo.

"We need to get Bre out of the meadow! I'm redirecting a helicopter to land in the meadow for extraction ASAP. She NEEDS to be monitoring this frequency. I can't make contact; can anybody reach her? We have to get her out!"

Having no idea who this was on the radio I responded on the same air-to-ground frequency by saying, *This is Bre in the meadow. Go ahead.*

To which, the person I assumed to be Air Attack quickly came back informing me that he'd be landing an aircraft for my extraction. I let him know that I was comfortable in the safety zone, and that there was already an extraction plan in place. I'm not sure whether the commo broke out while I was talking, or he just didn't have confidence in what I was saying, but the result was the same. A helicopter was inbound to the meadow and already in view, like it or not.

As it got closer, I realized that it was a state helicopter with the bucket and longline still attached, which added some complexity. Being a federal employee, per fire aviation rules, I was not allowed to ride in that aircraft. Then there are even more fire aviation rules forbidding someone from riding in a helicopter with the bucket and longline attached... *so there's that.*

Then of course, after all my lugging of gear, the helicopter landed on the exact opposite side of the meadow from where I had stacked everything for pick-up; *perfect.*

I approached the helicopter, flung open the door, and in my loudest -over the rotorwash- holler asked the pilot if he'd like me to disconnect the bucket and longline. He shook his head no, so I let him know I'd be grabbing some gear before we took off. I got an 'OK' head nod, and so began my shuttle sprint across the meadow.

In the grand scheme of things, fire gear isn't that big of a deal. Even if it were to get burned up it's all replace-able. The gear was in a perfectly safe place to ride out the fire, (which was now beginning to encircle the meadow) but my concern had more to do with the rappeller belly bags. Belly bags are bulky gear bags that rappellers end up using to keep their personal items like wallets, phones, flight helmets, rappel harnesses, extra clothing, etc., while they're fighting fire. I didn't want people to be without those things until someone flew back for the gear pile, who knows when.

So, there I was, sprinting across the meadow with gear bags swinging wildly from each hand, helping to add a dash of awkwardness to the already challenging task. After a couple of gear shuttling trips back-and-forth, I flung open the door, stuffed it all inside and hopped in.

As we began to rise off the ground I thought, *"welp, this is a big no-no,"* ha! But what was I supposed to do? The aircraft was directed to come pick me up, and I was directed to get into the helicopter; the rest was rather inconsequential at the moment.

I was wearing my firefighting helmet rather than a flight helmet and therefore, had no communication with the pilot, which meant I had no idea where we were going. As we chugged along, I began to recognize that we were headed to Ellensburg, making for a longer ride. Upon landing, I started to unload the belly bags as a rappel spotter came zooming up in a UTV.

He slammed it into park while simultaneously hopping out with a look of panicked relief and said, "Are you okay?!?"

Not fully understanding the level of concern, I responded pretty casually.

Well, as it turns out, I'd missed quite a bit of radio commo which apparently made it seem as if I were in grave danger.

I explained the chain of events as we drove across the tarmac and over to the helicopter crew. Once we got to the crew I experienced the same concerned reaction, so I again explained what happened in the field. Then, all of a sudden, my body sent me a very clear message. The message was, *"Haaangrrryyyy."*

It wasn't until that moment that it occurred to me, I had essentially been participating in the fireline Olympics all day long with categories including long distance-fast paced hiking (weighted), hurdles, squats, dead lifts, and farmer's carry. All while being fueled by approximately two measly packages of fruit snacks that I had tucked into my cargo pocket that morning. Not surprisingly, they didn't sustain my body from the billion or so calories I had burned off.

Not two minutes after receiving the *hangry* message I received a phone call from the unit aviation officer wanting to know what happened. I explained yet *again*, as I walked to the other side of the tarmac to hop in a rig and find some food. As I was finishing that phone call, I was met by a group of four guys; a traveling STAT team, who wanted me to explain what happened and then sit down to write a personal account of the events.

Fortunately, I knew one of the guys personally so it was slightly less jarring when I let loose a spattering of profanities which was my attempt at telling them if I didn't get some food in the very near future I was going to come completely unhinged. The message was received, and I was graced with a short window of time to stuff my face, which significantly improved my willingness to tell the story over again verbally, *and in writing.*

I wish I could say that was the last time I had to explain what happened, but over the next several days I had to re-tell the events virtually on repeat to an endless stream of people, which ended up being exponentially more exhausting than that day out in the field hurdling over logs and power lifting boxes of gear.

Of course, I had a question of my own that I wanted answered. I wanted to know why there was such a panic about pulling me out of our safety zone? Eventually I got an answer. As it turns out, the person I talked to over the radio wasn't Air Attack, but a lead plane operator. Apparently, the lead plane briefly filled in for the Air Attack platform, and that's when I was spotted and panic ensued.

Without the same level of fire experience as an Air Attack, the lead plane operator saw my position and, assuming I was in danger, reacted the best way they knew how.

All in all, everything worked out fine but I definitely could have done without multiple days of questioning, especially since the day after the incident happened to be my birthday. However, the crew surprised me with a birthday cake which had frosting art that depicted me riding in a helicopter with a bucket attached. So, at least I could have my cake and eat it too!

Isaak Sager

"YEP, WE'RE ON A FIRE. IT'S HOT."

There's a fire out there and we're comin' in hot

There's work to be done and it's probably a lot

We're diggin' in dirt, suckin' in ash, and eatin' up smoke like it ain't no joke

Just cuttin' through trees like we're the breeze

We're called firefighters and we're a helluva breed

Always up to the task to help those in need

We rappel out of choppers and jump out of planes, and roll in big trucks down highway lanes

From coast to coast, desert to the woods, we go round and round, nature is our hood

Just keep a watchful eye, for yourself and your bud, cause
the 10s and 18s are written in blood

Riva Duncan

ATTENTION!

Location: Washington
Year: 2001

Firefighters learn which food caterers are the best and which are... not. Word spreads. But in busy fire years, it's not uncommon to have more fires than available caterers. This can go either really well or very, very wrong.

My first experience with that was not a happy one. I was on a fire in Northern Washington in 2001. It was a busy fire season and, sure enough, no more caterers. We were told the incident management team (IMT) found a food provider at the local carnival.

The meals weren't horrible – lunches were pretty basic, a couple of meat and cheese sandwiches for the carnivores (PB&J for the vegetarians), fruit, granola bars, candy. Then one morning an urgent announcement came over the radio to everyone on the fire.

"Attention to all personnel on the fire. Do not eat the meat sandwiches in the lunches. Repeat. Do not eat the meat sandwiches in the lunches."

Of course, folks with meat lunches immediately opened them to see what the issue was. The roast beef wasn't green (common). The bread wasn't moldy (happens). Nope. It was worms! *Worms* in the meat. People were gagging, yelling, throwing sandwiches, and joking about their bonus protein.

As I watched the whole scene play out, I thought to myself, *this is why firefighters carry their own food stashes!*

CHAPTER 5

Fire Season's Curtain Call

"Every fire is born to die."
- Courtney McGee

Logbook for the PT hike of fire crews and local community members. Entiat, WA.

Sara Sweeney

MIMBRES MEMORIES

Location: Black Fire, Mimbres, New Mexico
Year: 2022

It's been many years since I've been here, maybe 2011? The Miller Fire, another fire deep in the Gila Wilderness that probably didn't need to be put out; I was a scrappy squad leader on a Northwest hotshot crew, still just trying to figure out what I was doing with my life. Sometimes, I'm still not sure I know.

Waiting to fly into the fire, watching one of our sister crews fly off and wondering what we were getting into… watching them stumble off the helicopter into the dust shaking their heads, just grateful to be back on flat ground, telling us we were in for "a doozy."

We spent eight days in a spike camp in a saddle at 8000' feet, hiking every day to our work area through a wind that refused to quit, even in the chilly starlit evenings when the winds in the Southwest tend to diminish, I remember it howling through the night as if punishing us. Astounded by the scenery around me, I kept thinking just how odd our job really is. Sheer rock faces and jaw-dropping cliffs, views of the least populated places in the country... and to sweeten the deal, only the finest government cuisine–three MREs a day and all the lukewarm water you can drink.

Location: Mimbres Fire, Mimbres, New Mexico
Year: 2022

I had forgotten just how big the Gila is.

The spaces stretch out in every direction like an unrolling canvas, endless and empty, the hills undulating under their juniper cover, tawny with grass. The valleys between start small and harmless-looking, burrowing back into the mountains until suddenly you are in a cleft so deep it seems you are descending into the earth itself, with the steepness of God on either side and the sun overhead baking your skin. Not a breath of wind. These hills and valleys grow and mature into mountains, rocky faces looming on the skyline as thunderstorms build and roil across the sky.

Then there is the sky itself.

Bright blue against the dark green and shimmering grass, in midsummer the clouds begin to puff up and gather around midday, signaling their call to arms. They darken and coalesce, gathering strength and growing heavy with moisture until they begin to shed, virga at first and doing no good for anyone by throwing lightning and discarding all reason with erratic winds that only push everything around. But as June marches toward July, they become more insistent; the bottoms of the clouds grow heavy and drop into Mammatus formations and the rain falls—lightly at first and then with a vengeance, washing everything clean of the dust that rises in the months between the melting snow and the monsoons.

It is like being born.

And the stars... the night sky stealing its own show again, and again, as the panoply of the constellations unfolds each night, the stars suddenly brighter without the light and noise of humans to interrupt them. The Milky Way winds through it all, arching on the darkness and reminding us of our mortality, and our unimportance.

Betsy Booth

SEPTEMBER 3 AT 8402'

Scorched ground
A forest of snags still standing
Maybe Flossie Fire? 10 years past, at least
September-dry brown desiccated
Lupine penstemon knotweed and grouseberry
One fireweed still blooming backlit brilliant
Early sun soaks into my back
blood sings in my ears, with no fire
and snow in the forecast tomorrow I've
gone off script, off the lookout
after check-in hour
radio silent on my belt
I'm sinking pier blocks into the ground
of this summer as
shards of light fall off each day
tilting far past solstice
and accelerating toward
dark at 4 pm
When I'll reach back here
Wolves singing in Sleepy Hollow

Kate Averett

SEASONED

There were many days when I wanted to quit. Yet, there were many more when I couldn't picture being anywhere else. I started a fire job four days after my eighteenth birthday, three days after I graduated high school. I remember being offered both a timber marking and a wildland fire position near the end of my senior year. My parents nudged me towards the timber marking job, the "safer" option, so, naturally, I took the job in fire.

I remember feeling thoroughly confused and being handed horribly ugly, oversized, dark green pants, and some dirty-looking, button-down yellow shirts–"Nomex" they called them. I remember lacing up my White's leather boots for the first time (which were ironically black) not quite tight enough, but still blisteringly uncomfortable. I remember how no matter which way I placed my hard hat on my head it somehow always remained crooked. I remember wearing my pack around for the first whole day, fairly empty compared to the weight I'd carry in the years to come, and feeling the twinge of new experiences seep into my knees then run down my shins, and over my ankles, before settling into my feet.

I remember early morning PTs, racing up the hill knowing the top was always just "two more chains" away, and crew runs that seemed fun only after they were over. I remember the excitement of a fire call- the tangible adrenaline, the increased heartbeat thudding against the backs of my wide eyes, flames glinting in their reflection. Fire is truly indescribable. Not just the way the orange glow dances across the landscape changing it from green to black, but the way lifelong friendships are forged, camaraderie becomes irreplaceable, and your crew becomes your second family. The days were generally long, the nights sometimes felt even longer, and usually, one, if not both, were accompanied by hikes with no real end in sight.

During my first 14-day dispatch we had been trudging up the slope, then down, and back up, and back down, and then for reassurance, back up another ten or so times and back down, and so on, filling the time and space of long August days. At times, the temperature reached well over 100 degrees, even the trees were sweating. The crew was chock-full of rookies and first-timers like me that had never been out on a dispatch before, but there were those that were veterans at this point, and they weren't much for putting up with any of our shit.

I remember Baker wordlessly hoisting the chainsaw over her shoulder and marching on. No words wasted. No breath lost. A college cross country star standing not far above 5 feet tall, packing enough pounds on her back to almost double her weight. She was close to thirty, with nearly a decade over me in fire experience, knowledge, and life, it seemed nothing could slow her down.

It was sometime during my first dispatch that I learned Kayla packed "lippers." I remember the chew; the realization that women did that too. I remember her leading the squad with ease, strength, and poise. Softly and with a strong arm. The honor of her presence was one you both enjoyed being in and worked hard to gain.

I was a mere 18, innocent, unknowing, and unsure of what I was even doing standing amidst a sea of trees in the blue mountains. But after a few days of witnessing these ladies and others in action, the standard had been set.

Fast forward seven years, and I'm bouncing along another dirt road, dark column overhead. Complete normalcy at this point- the scene, the work, the chaos. My squad boss feeds me the game plan from the driver's seat- where to scout, where to start saws, tools needed, radio frequencies to use. Gear up. Line out. Make a snarky comment. Hike. Go to work. Take a break. Crack a joke. Grab a bite.

Get back to work. Hike some more. Repeat for 100 or more days until the fire season subsides.

The crew life is something you only understand once you've experienced it. The long hours bleed into days that bleed into nights, then weeks, then months. The forced family you'll never be able to shake, and as the years go on, you'll be thankful that you never could.

And in twenty or so years, I'll think back to those nights. Maybe as I sit by a campfire that crackles and pops, the size of something that'd barely raise a concern or be called a spot fire most days, I'll think back to the spine-tingling "whoosh" of torching trees, the lapping of flames at our pant legs chasing our heels like dogs, and the delirious smiles we shared as yet another shift ended. I'll think back to the positives, the better memories, and the way fire molded me much like a blacksmith does iron. I might not remember, or rather choose to block out the long months of relentless hours, or the struggles that curtail the excitement of the off-season. But by the end, I think it'll all have been worth it. Every hike. Every roll. Every season. I'll regale how I left not being the same person that entered- character, work ethic, grit, and more, all altered by the hours of wearing a heavy pack or tromping another mile in blister-footed boots. And I'll be thankful for this job, the time I put in, the friendships forged, and all that it brought my way.

These are the moments I'll never forget, and the folks I'll be glad to have been surrounded by.

Taylor Kress

SUMMER'S ENDING

Now that Summer's ending
  I can stop my pretending

Imaginative figurines still face from the East
  And march in line with fat foot steps

They left homes, heartaches, and hurried goodbyes
  Only to see the same stark stance in each other's eyes

The drive was just beginning
  Miles and months more seemed to sit ahead
    Atop a bleak hill heavy, hammered and red

The Summer did come and go
  Same as the monsoons
    Leaving their watermarks, burn scars, and half
    hummed tunes

Kate Averett

WEATHERED

The rampant ash storm
That had been stirring for well over a week
Finally settled onto their cheeks
Merging with the dirt of days past

They now existed in a grey-scale
of told time.
Sodden skin blended sweat and soot
Shading faces
Like smoke smothers the sun

As the end to long days approach
Smiles of vivacious white teeth erupt
The only pieces left untarnished
By the chaos that fire brings

I KNOW THIS PLACE

I know this place.

I was dropped here by a helicopter.

I have hiked this ridgeline every day for nearly two weeks now.

I dug a flat sleep spot, mined out all the lumpy rocks, and built a pillow out of dirt; my bed.

I have moved up and down these slopes each day, imprinting all I see, hear, feel and smell.

I know this place.

I know the texture of the dirt we've been digging in day after day.

I know the time of day by the way the sun casts its rays on

the ashen ground.

I know the knob is up ahead, and that the drop point is a five-minute hike further past that.

I know that there's a half burned-out snag up slope and just to the right of my current location.

I know these people.

I know the stride of the person ahead of me in line order.

I know your habits, your pet peeves, and your favorite things.

I know who will wake first and who will scramble to get ready.

I know the sleeping slouch of the person who sits in front of me in the buggies.

I know these people.

I know the sounds of a crew hard at work.

I know everyone's unspoken, yet claimed space around the warming fire each morning.

I know the quiet cadence of every single crew as they crest a ridgeline in the wilderness.

I know you by the tilt of your helmet, the sag of your fire pack, and your echoing laugh.

I know this place, and I'll know it forever.

I know these people, and I'll know them forever.

Moonlighting

Something I've noticed that seems to permeate through the wildland fire community is exceptional talent and creativity; there certainly is no shortage of gifted and artistic people who lend their hand to all variety of craft-trades. It wouldn't be uncommon to meet a wildland firefighter who practices blacksmithing, leatherwork, sewing, beading, weaving, knitting, welding, chainsaw art, apothecary, pottery throwing, glass blowing, etc. Afterall, working with our hands is second nature.

Because this is such a common thread that runs through the fire family, I feel that it's important to make space in each volume of *Hold and Improve* to highlight firefighter-owned, craft-trade businesses. It's a nice way for these business owners to receive a little more notice and support, but it also provides a space for them to tell their story while giving recognition to this aspect of the fire culture.

Owner: D.B. Robbins

PASTIME LEATHER CO.

Location: Twisp, WA

Pastime Leather Co. began in the offseason (winter) of 2015. Leatherwork began as a creative outlet, and I quickly found that concentrating on something other than my day job was extremely beneficial to my mental wellbeing. I started out hand cutting, then saddle-stitching each item. This method doesn't require a bunch of fancy or expensive equipment- just the will to learn, and to be ok with the inherent mistakes that come with the process. Each of the steps involved require the utmost care and attention to detail. One lapse in concentration, and the project usually ends up suplexed into the scrap bin, or perhaps used for target practice. Fairly recently, I bit the bullet and acquired a leather sewing machine, which allows me to produce very high-quality work while still keeping prices reasonable.

If you are reading this thinking to yourself, "I would like to do something like that but… (enter excuse here)," just take the first step. It can be challenging, but people in our line of work are not particularly known for backing down from a challenge.

You can find me at:

Website: www.pastimeleatherco.com
Instagram: pastime_leather_co
Email: pastimehandbuilt@gmail.com

ANCHOR AND FLANK CANDLES

Location: Aiken, South Carolina

Anchor and Flank Candles began during the off-season between 2021 and 2022. I had just come off my first season on an engine – my third season in fire – and was looking for my next challenge. Mind you, I never anticipated starting a business. But, then again, I never anticipated getting involved with wildland fire either, and here I am, having done both of those things. It's funny where life takes you, isn't it?

From its inception, Anchor and Flank Candles was intended to be a hand-poured candle business that revolved around, and gave back to, the wildland fire community. Specifically, I had this crazy idea to create candles themed around the wildland fire lifestyle and then donate a portion of the profits to injured wildland firefighters. In addition, I decided to donate candles to fundraisers that bring in even more funds than my business could on its own. In the winter of 2021, my now-husband and I set to work, fashioning the scent profiles after smells within wildland fire while tying into some comical, idiomatic candle names. Each candle is crafted with a wooden wick, hand-poured in a metal tin, and meant to bring laughter, love and light to whoever burns it.

In its two years of business, Anchor and Flank Candles has become so much more than a small candle business; it's become a sort of catalyst for community, and that is what truly sets my soul on fire.

What started out as a personal challenge and an idea to help my community, has grown into so much more, and I am continually amazed by the love and support from folks in wildland fire. To the person reading this who is sitting on an idea that you're too scared or nervous to share... please, share it with the world. Don't be afraid of taking that leap of faith, because you truly never know where life can take you, if you let it.

Love and Light,

Danna

Find Anchor and Flank here:

Website: www.anchorandflankcandles.com
Email: anchorandflankcandles@gmail.com
Facebook, Instagram, Pinterest, TikTok, and YouTube

Fire Lingo Glossary

AGL (Above Ground Level): AGL is an aviation reference. Example: Smokejumpers who use round parachutes exit the aircraft at 1,500 ft AGL, versus square chute jumpers who exit at 3,000 ft AGL.

Aerial Ignition: An ignition method where essentially flaming ping pong balls are dropped from a helicopter in specific patterns to help firefighters on the ground burn out large geographic areas.

AFMO (Assistant Fire Management Officer): An FMO manages the fire resources on a fire district. An AFMO is the position below the FMO. Example: A fire district has three engines and one handcrew, the FMO (or possibly AFMO) is their supervisor.

After Action Review (AAR): A formal or informal debriefing process of an event. The focus is to improve performance, while openly discussing the positives and negatives that may have taken place during said event.

Agency Administrator (AA): A person within the chain of command who has ultimate responsibility for an incident or geographic area. The fire chain of command will fall under an AA.

Air Attack (ATGS): Typically a fixed-wing aircraft is used to fly the air attack qualified personnel over an incident. The ATGS acts as an eye-in-the-sky to assist personnel on the ground with a different perspective of the incident, while also coordinating the incoming and outgoing aircraft above the fire.

Air Tanker: A plane (fixed-wing aircraft) that drops fire retardant.

Annual Leave: Annual leave is part of the vacation pay system for federal employees. An employee will accrue a few hours off per pay period, which builds up over time.

Aspect: The cardinal direction that a slope is facing. For example: If you are standing on a slope looking outward across the landscape, and the direction that you are looking is south, it means you are on the southern aspect.

Auger In: A commonly used phrase with aerially delivered firefighters, especially helicopter rappellers. It refers to generating too much speed on your descent and hitting the ground hard enough to hurt yourself.

Backburn: A fire that is set to burn away from your location with the wind.

Back Cut: When using a conventional cut to take down a tree with a chainsaw the sawyer would first cut a wedge out of the tree, called the "face cut." After the face cut has been made, the sawyer would then move the saw to the backside of the tree and make a back cut, which is what will make the tree fall.

Backing Fire: A fire that is burning against the wind and/or downslope is usually referred to as a *backing fire.*

Belt Weather Kit: A tool used by firefighters to take weather observations on an hourly basis throughout the day. Taking weather observations may also be referred to as slinging weather.

Bladder Bag: A backpack that is specifically designed to carry water. The backpack comes with a pump-action wand, which attaches to the backpack and allows the user to spray water onto hotspots. A full bladder bag generally weighs around 45 lbs. *Also referred to as a piss pump.*

Bone Pile: When firefighters take pieces of burning logs from within a section of the fire and pile them together (in a safe spot) so that they burn hot and cause complete consumption, that is referred to as a *bone pile.*

Box Canyon: A steep-sided, dead-end canyon.

Bucket: A collapsible bucket that attaches to the belly of a helicopter with a longline. The helicopter pilot dips the bucket into a water source and drops the water on flared-up areas of the fire. This is referred to as a "bucket drop."

Bucking: When a sawyer cuts a downed tree into smaller, more manageable chunks, or "rounds."

Buddy Check: A system check used with aerially delivered firefighters to ensure that all components of their life-bearing equipment have been properly configured. Two people come together and perform the check on one another.

Buggy: The boxy hotshot vehicles which can carry 10 people and a significant amount of fire gear are referred to as buggies.

Build Up: Or "Cell Build Up" is a reference to cumulus clouds building in the sky, which could be a sign of thunderstorms later in the day. Thunderstorm cells generate significant downdrafts and can create severe conditions on a wildfire. Storm cells are considered a serious watch-out for firefighters.

Bump:
1. Take a bump- This refers to moving up the distance of one person while building a fireline. It means that line construction is easier than it needs to be at the back of the line and the people in the front can move ahead to give them more work.
2. Bumping into the Green- Going to the bathroom outside of the fire perimeter. It is a cardinal sin to go to the bathroom in "the black" because firefighters put their bare hands in the ashen ground to search for areas that are holding heat.

Burnout: Setting a fire in order to consume fuel between the edge of the wildfire and the fireline. A burnout provides firefighters a bit more control of the fire behavior happening near the fireline, rather than allowing the wildfire to approach the fireline, and possibly move past it.

Burnover: A circumstance where firefighters become trapped by intense fire behavior with no way out. This is when a firefighter would deploy their fire shelter as a last resort for survival. The fire would then *burn over* them while they were inside their fire shelter.

Burn Scar: When a fire has burned through an area, the remnants are referred to by firefighters as a burn scar. For example, you might plan to let a fire burn up to the edge of the Tumwater fire burn scar because the fire will die out with no fuel to consume.

Cache: A storage area for firefighter supplies and equipment.

Canopy: The top portion of a tree where the leaves and/or needles reside.

Catface: When fire burns a concave into a tree's trunk, making the tree unstable that is called a catface.

Cargo Box: A box of firefighting supplies that either gets lowered from a helicopter (for rappellers), or released from an airplane (for smokejumpers). Cargo boxes include all the necessary firefighting equipment such as tools, chainsaw, fuel, medical kit, food, water, and miscellaneous supplies. A cargo box may also be referred to as a fire box and/or saw box, each holding their specified respective gear.

Cargo Chute: The type/size parachute that is specifically used for cargo boxes.

Cargo Drop: The aerial mission of releasing cargo out of an aircraft to deliver it to firefighters on the ground.

Cargo Letdown: The act of a spotter letting a cargo box down from a helicopter to the ground.

Ceiling: Ceiling is a term used in aviation that references the cloud level. Example: The ceiling is too low for the helicopter to fly.

Chain: A measure of distance, which is 66 ft. A chain is commonly referenced when building a fireline, and firefighters generally know how many of their own paces would equal one chain.

Chain of Command: The hierarchy of management levels within the firefighting organization. The chain of command is closely adhered to in firefighting. Hotshot Crew Example (Top to bottom): Superintendent, foreman, squad leader, senior firefighter, firefighter. If there is an issue you go upward in the chain of command one rung at a time until the issue has been resolved.

Chaparral: Chaparral is a thick, dense, shrub.

Chase Truck: The term is used interchangeably with a vehicle that carries crew supplies and equipment, or the vehicle that the overhead rides in. For helitack and rappel crews the chase truck is the vehicle that follows the helicopter to its final destination. It carries additional crewmembers and equipment to set up a helibase.

Check Line: A temporary fireline that is constructed in order to contain the fire while other tactics are being implemented, or additional resources are en route.

Chick Stick: *See Stick definition.* A chick stick is when both firefighters in the stick are women. Due to the low number of women in wildland firefighting, a chick stick tends to be rare.

Cliffed-Out: Working on wildfires in diverse terrain can sometimes find firefighters in a position where they come up against a cliff's edge, thereby hampering their efforts to move forward/down/up depending on the circumstance.

Climbers Left/Right: Generally used to describe a location when talking on the radio. Example: "The snag that needs to be cut down is upslope from your location by about 100 ft., climber's right."

Cold Front: A cold air mass moving in, displacing the warmer air. A forecasted cold front is a watch-out situation for firefighters because the wind intensifies and shifts directions, creating unpredictable and potentially extreme fire behavior.

Cold Trail: There are some fuel types that simply burn out with no real chance of spreading. In circumstances like these, firefighters will de-glove and run the backside of their hand along the burned edge of the fire, to feel for heat. It is a way to move quickly along the fire's edge so that focus can be placed on the areas that need real attention.

Column: The smoke plume that is visible above a fire is a column.

Comms: *Communications.* Aerial firefighters plug in and out of a *comms box* in the aircraft by the cord attached to their flight helmets. It's generally much too loud to communicate inside aircraft without using the avionics system.

Conduction: The transfer of heat through direct contact.

Contingency Line: A secondary fireline that is created as a backup when there is concern over the ability to hold the original fireline. Contingency line is essentially Plan B.

Contract Crews: While the majority of fire crews are either state or federal employees, there is also a sizeable portion of private industry fire resources who are hired contractually.

Convection: The transfer of heat by movement of a gas or liquid.

Creeping: Low fire intensity. When small flames "creep"

along the forest floor burning surface fuels.

Crowning: *or Crown Fire.* When a fire is moving along in the tops of the trees completely independent of fire on the forest floor.

Cubee: A plastic bladder of drinking water encased in a cardboard box, which comes with a plastic handle for carrying. Firefighters typically slide the cubee onto their tool handle using the plastic handle to hike it to their work location. The standard volume of a cubee is 5 gallons, but smokejumpers and rappellers may pack 2.5 gallon cubees.

Cumulus Build-Up: Normally, cumulus clouds are not a concern for firefighters. However, when build-up turns into a cumulonimbus (tall anvil-shaped cloud), firefighters pay close attention, due to the potential for sudden downdrafts and gusty winds, which can dramatically affect fire behavior.

Cup Trench: When a fire is on a steep slope and there is danger of burning material rolling further down the slope and igniting a fire below, there is a need for a cup trench. A cup trench is built underneath the fire's edge on the downhill side. It is a deep v-shaped trench that is wide enough to catch rolling debris from the fire.

Cutting Line: Building/constructing fireline.

Daisy Chain: A way to transport something using multiple connected links.

DBH (Diameter Breast Height): DBH is a term used when falling a tree. It refers to the circumference of a tree at breast height.

Dead and Down: Areas that have a significant amount of dead trees lying on the forest floor. The downed trees are usually crisscrossed and stacked on top of one another. This is commonly referred to as Jackstraw, Jim-Jam, or *Dead and Down.*

Dead Man's Curve: An aviation term that refers to the increased danger level of certain missions based on a calculation that accounts for height from the ground (AGL), and airspeed. Many common wildland fire missions happen within the *Dead Man's Curve.*

Demob: When a firefighter or fire resource (e.g. engine crew, hotshot crew) is leaving an incident due to lack of necessity or fulfilling their 14-day assignment they go through the "demob" process. *Demobilization; officially checking out of the fire to begin travel home.

Descent Device: Helicopter rappellers use a rope and "descent device" to lower themselves from the helicopter to the ground.

Diggers: Crewmembers with hand tools who physically dig in the ground to construct a fireline. In a "line dig," firefighters are generally broken into two groups, the saws, and the diggers.

Direct Attack: Working to put the fire out along the fire's edge.

Dispatch: Fire dispatchers assign fire resources to respond to new fires, while also documenting fire size-ups relayed from the field, tracking firefighters' whereabouts, coordinating aircraft to respond to multiple fire incidents, and much more.

Division (DIVS):
1. A division is a geographical piece of ground. Large wildfires get broken up into divisions, which helps make a fire easier to manage. Fire resources then report to their respective *division*.
2. Division is also a qualified fire position. Each division

of a fire has a division supervisor who manages the fire resources on that portion of the fire. Referred to as *Division,* or DIVS Sup.

Dolmar: A fuel container that has a compartment for chainsaw fuel, as well as bar oil.

Dozer Line: A fireline that has been created by a bulldozer.

Dozer Operator: Bulldozers are used regularly in firefighting operations. Dozer operators need to be very skilled in order to navigate the difficult terrain, as well as the additional hazards associated with wildfire.

Drip Torch: A firing device used regularly by firefighters in burnout operations. A drip torch is a handheld metal can (approximately 15-20 lbs when full) with a long wick to drip fuel. Firefighters ignite the wick and literally drip fire onto the ground as they hike along.

Dry Run: Before a retardant plane makes a drop, a dry run is performed to show the intended path and placement.

Dual Career: If both partners in a relationship have a fire career it's referred to as *dual career.*

Duff: The layer of decomposing leaf litter that sits just above the mineral soil layer. Fire can smolder in duff for a long time, given the opportunity.

Duty Officer (DO): A person who is the on-call point of contact for dispatch if there is a reported smoke (fire). The DO will then either go scout the smoke themselves or have dispatch send fire resources to assess the situation.

Eddy: Circling air or water that resides on the backside of a solid obstacle such as a mountain ridgeline, or large boulder in a river is called an *eddy.*

ELT: *Emergency Locator Transmitter.* An ELT is affixed to aircraft in case of a hard landing or crash.

Engine Crews: An engine crew generally consists of 3-7 people who usually work along road systems. Engine crews are invaluable in the "urban interface" setting when structures (homes, buildings, etc.) are being threatened by an advancing wildfire.

Entrapment: When firefighters have been enclosed by a fire with no way out. An entrapment may, or may not necessitate the use of fire shelters.

ERC Chart: *Energy Release Component* Chart. ERC Charts are used by firefighters to reference historical fire activity relative to weather and dryness of fuel, based on the date.

Escape Route: A pre-established route that has been flagged and made clear of obstacles so that firefighters can quickly leave the area they are working and make way to the safety zone if necessary.

Face Cut: When using a conventional cut to fall a tree with a chainsaw the sawyer would first cut a wedge out of the tree, called the "face cut." After the face cut has been made, the sawyer would then move the saw to the backside of the tree and make a back cut, which is what will make the tree fall.

Faller: A person who has been trained and certified to cut down trees. There are different levels of certification, from novice to highly experienced. Firefighters may be qualified to cut down hazardous trees as well.

Fine Fuels: Fine fuels are essentially the kindling to a forest fire. They are the easiest to catch fire and will generate enough heat to help catch heavier fuels on fire. Fine fuels are also referred to as light flashy fuels. Strong winds mixed with light flashy fuels can be quite dangerous and/or destructive.

Fingers: Depending on the way a fire burns it may burn in such a way as to create "fingers." Typically, firefighters will burnout a section of unburned fuel to make the fire's circumference more circular. Dealing with long fingers on a fire expends much more time and effort for firefighters.

Firebrand: A firebrand is a burning ember that has the potential to ignite unburned fuel if it is blown across the fireline into "the green."

Firebreak: An area that is cleared of combustible fuel. A firebreak (or fuel break) can be human-created or natural.

Fireline: A fireline is similar in appearance to a hiking trail. A fireline encircles a fire and removes the ability of the fire to continue spreading by digging/scraping away fuel down to the mineral soil layer. The width of a fireline will vary greatly depending on the fuel type, topography, and fire behavior.

Fire Assignment: When a firefighter leaves on an out-of-area fire assignment, more than likely that person will be gone for at least 14 days. Firefighters could get extended to 21 days if there's a need. Another possibility is that after working for 14 days, the fire crew could take "R+R" days in area local to the fire before working an additional 14 days, and then returning home.

Fire Camp: Fire camp is essentially a tent city. Fire camp and ICP (incident command post) can sometimes be used interchangeably, but they are not always in the same location as one another. Fire camp provides resources for firefighters such as food, supplies, and designated sleeping areas, while ICP is wherever the IMT (incident management team) has set up their command post.

Fire Gear: Also referred to as line gear, line pack, or fire pack. Essentially, fire gear is the fire backpack that is worn on the fireline. However, fire gear may also encompass PPE like boots, helmet, and a tool.

Fire Triangle: The fire triangle consists of the three components necessary to make a fire-fuel, heat, and oxygen.

Fire Scar: When a fire has burned through an area, the

remnants are referred to by firefighters as a fire scar, and/
or burn scar. Example: you might plan to let a fire burn
up to the edge of the Tumwater fire scar because the fire
will die out with no fuel to consume.

Fire Season: The time of year when weather aligns with
dry forest vegetation is fire season. Fire season takes
place at different times of the year depending on the geographic region of the country/world. With each passing
year fire season is expanding due to warmer climates
and dry vegetation turning fire season into more of a "fire
year."

Fire Shelter: A lifesaving piece of PPE carried by American wildland firefighters as a last resort tool. If a firefighter was on the verge of being burned over by a fire, they
could deploy this multi-layered heat shield, and crawl
inside in an attempt to survive the flaming front and
super-heated gases.

Fire Qualifications: A person's fire qualifications are
listed on their "red card." Qualifications are gained after a
firefighter has taken the appropriate classes and successfully completed the "taskbook" associated with the qualification. Fire qualifications are also referred to as quals.

Fire Whirl: Essentially a fire tornado that has the potential to carry debris, smoke, and flame over the fireline and into unburned fuel. Fire whirls can vary greatly in size.

Firing Operation: When firefighters intentionally light a fire for a specific purpose.

Flank: A wildfire has a head, two flanks, and the heel. The flanks are either side of the fire.

Flare Up: A flare-up usually occurs when the surface fire has been pre-heating ladder fuels and they finally dry and begin to catch fire.

Flight Following: The process through which an aircraft is tracked from departure point to destination. Flight following provides the aircraft's location at regular time intervals in case of an event or mishap. This way, the aircraft can be located quickly during the search and rescue. Additionally, Automated Flight Following (AFF) is a system in which the aircraft is followed via computer tracker so that the dispatcher (or person following the flight) can see the aircraft's location on a map.

Flight Suit: A coverall type outfit that is worn over clothing during flights.

FMO (Fire Management Officer): An FMO manages the fire resources on a fire district. Example: A fire district has three engines and one handcrew, the FMO is their supervisor.

Foehn Wind: A warm, dry, and strong seasonal wind that takes place in certain geographical areas. A wind of this type can create critical fire weather conditions. Foehn winds are called by different names according to the geographic location; such as Santa Ana winds in Southern California.

Fold-a-Tank: A Fold-A-Tank is a collapsible water storage system that can be transported by truck or helicopter to remote locations, in order to provide firefighters with a water source.

Food Box/Bag: A food box/bag is a food supply provided to smokejumpers and rappellers that should last each firefighter 72 hours.

Foreman: Second in command on a fire crew.

Fresh Food Box: A large box of fresh food ingredients is provided regularly via cargo drop to firefighters in the backcountry of Alaska.

Fuel:
1. Combustible material, which includes vegetation such as grass, leaves, ground litter, plants, shrubs, and trees. All of which fuel a wildfire.
2. Fuel: Actual fuel used for chainsaws, water pumps, etc.

Fuel Cycle: Fuel cycle is an aviation term. In wildfire, it's used to reference the duration of time a pilot can work for you. Example: When a helicopter arrives on scene, the firefighter might ask over the radio, "where are you in your fuel cycle?" and the pilot will respond with an approximation of how much longer they can fly before having to set down the aircraft to refuel.

Fuel Moisture Content: A calculated percentage of water content found in vegetation. The fuel moisture content lets firefighters know how available fuel is to burn. The less fuel moisture, the higher the fire danger.

Fusee: A strikeable flare that is commonly carried in fireline packs and used in small-scale firing operations.

Fuselage: The main body of an aircraft.

GACC: Geographic Area Coordination Center.

Green: Being green refers to a new firefighter. A rookie firefighter. *See:* "The Green" for additional definition.

Greens: Firefighters often refer to their Nomex fire pants as their *greens.* Nomex pants are a PPE requirement for the fireline.

Gridding: *Or Grid* is a formal search formation. In fire, a grid formation is generally used to walk through an unburned area looking for spot fires or to search through a burned area for remaining heat/smoke.

Haines Index: An index that is referenced by firefighters to help them predict potential fire growth. The Haines Index functions on a scale that measures between 2-6; 6 being the highest potential for large fire growth.

H-pay: Hazard pay is referred to as H-pay. H-pay is an additional pay bump that is granted when engaged on a wildfire.

Handcrew: A group of approximately 10-20 firefighters who work together consistently throughout the fire season. Typically, firefighters continue to work on the same crew for several years in a row.

Handline: A fireline built with hand tools.

Head of the Fire: The side of the fire with the fastest rate of spread.

Heavy Fuels: Larger circumference dead trees and logs are considered heavy fuels. Even if heavy fuels are dried out, they still require pre-heating before being able to catch fire.

Heel of the Fire: The back of the fire, opposite from the "head" of the fire.

Helibase: Helibase is essentially the incident command post for aviation resources. It is also the physical ground where rotor-wing aircraft (helicopters) that are assigned to a specific incident take off, land, and park overnight.

Helispot: A space in the forest that has been cleared to certain specifications so that a helicopter may land in the backcountry safely.

Helitack: Firefighters who utilize a helicopter as their mode of transportation to deliver them to a wildfire.

Hold and Improve:
1. A command used during fireline construction, which signifies the need to stop forward progress.
2. Slang for "sit around and wait for an undetermined amount of time." Find something to keep you busy for awhile.

Holder: A firefighter who is standing on the fireline looking for spot fires while a burnout operation is going on.

Holdover Fire: Lightning storms that produce ground strikes can start fires. It's not unusual for a fire to smolder, not showing smoke for several days, before finally being spotted by a fire lookout. This type of new start would be called a *holdover fire*.

Hose Lay: An extensive connection of several lengths of fire hose is called a hose lay. The hose gets carried into the forest by firefighters, then assembled on the ground beginning at the water source. The water source could be a fire engine, a fold-a-tank, a stream/river, etc.

Hotshot Crew: A 20+ person handcrew. Hotshot crews are required to maintain specific fitness levels and fire qualifications. Hotshot crews are a highly regarded, Type 1, firefighting resource.

Hung-Up Tree: When a tree has started to fall over but got stuck in the tops of other trees on its way down it is "hung up." This poses a hazard to firefighters since the base of the tree is not secure and the tree could break loose and come down at any time.

IA (Initial Attack): When a fire starts, the firefighters first on scene are considered to be the initial attack resource. In this circumstance, firefighters regularly say they are I.A.'ing a fire.

IA Crew: IA Fire crews are dispatched to be first on scene of a new fire.

IAP (Incident Action Plan): An IAP is used by firefighters on large incidents to reference communications plans, resources, maps, emergency medical information, etc.

IC (Incident Commander): The incident commander is the person in charge of a fire. The larger the fire is, an IC may have support staff under them, such as operations, plans, logistics, etc.

ICP (Incident Command Post): The ICP is the geographic location where an incident management team sets up its operations. The ICP is usually in the same place as "fire camp," which is essentially a base camp for firefighters.

ICS (Incident Command System): ICS is used to organize chaotic situations by establishing a chain of command, as well as parameters for workload, number of subordinates, etc.

IMT (Incident Management Team): An IMT is a group of specially qualified people to organize and maintain control of large fire incidents.

Indirect Attack: A method of fire suppression where a fireline is constructed far ahead of the fire's edge for the fire to eventually run into.

Inversion: An atmospheric condition that will cause smoke to settle into valleys, or low-lying areas until the inversion lifts. An inversion generally lifts by early-to-mid afternoon, but an inversion could remain for several days, creating issues for aviation resources.

IR: Infrared heat detection system.

IRPG (Incident Resource Pocket Guide): All firefighters carry an IRPG with them while fighting fire. It is a valuable quick guide commonly referenced for information such as proper helispot circumference, etc.

Island: An unburned area within a fire's perimeter (also known as a pocket) is referred to as an *island.*

Jackstraw: Areas that have a significant amount of dead trees lying on the forest floor. The downed trees are usually crisscrossed and stacked on top of one another. This is commonly referred to as *Jackstraw,* Jim-Jam, or Dead and Down.

Jet-A: Fuel used for aircraft.

Jim-Jam: Areas that have a significant amount of dead trees lying on the forest floor. The downed trees are usually crisscrossed and stacked on top of one another. This is commonly referred to as Jackstraw, *Jim-Jam,* or Dead and Down.

Jumper: Smokejumper.

Jump Gear: Smokejumper suit. Jump gear consists of

a large, bulky, pale-yellow suit made from Kevlar and hockey padding. Jump gear also includes a helmet (with face cage), flight gloves, a reserve, and a main parachute.

Jump Spot: The area that has been designated by the spotter as the place for smokejumpers to land.

Ladder Fuels: Mid-height fuels that help a fire go from ground/surface fuels, up to the tops of the trees are called *ladder fuels.*

LAL (Lightning Activity Level): LAL is part of the National Fire Danger Rating System (NFDRS) and is in reference to the probable frequency of cloud-to-ground lightning strikes.

LCES (Lookout-Communication-Escape Routes-Safety Zones): It is considered bad business to engage in a wildfire without first establishing these four safety measures.

Lead Plane: Aircraft/pilot that makes trial runs over the target areas of a fire prior to the air tanker itself. Lead planes also guide air tankers through a drop.

Letdown Lines: Tubular webbing that is used to lower cargo from an aircraft. Letdown line is also used by smokejumpers when they land in a tree. They use it to build a makeshift harness and lower themselves to the ground.

Lighter: A firefighter who is one of the people carrying a drip torch and dropping dots of fire in the forest during a burnout operation.

Lightning Bust: Lightning storms have the potential to create multiple new fires. When this happens, firefighters refer to it as a *lightning bust.*

Line: Shorthand for fireline.

Line Dig: The construction of a fireline by a group of people. A line dig could consist of any number of people depending on the circumstance.

Line gear/pack: A firefighter's backpack of gear, which is carried with them on the fireline at all times.

Line Order: Handcrews (especially hotshot crews) have an order in which crewmembers line up to dig fireline and/or hike. The order is generally kept the same for the entire fire season with few exceptions. This means that the people in front and back of you while you're in line, will always be the same. The order is developed based on which tool each person has been assigned and where it will be complementary in a line dig as compared to other tools.

Load:

1. A load of smokejumpers and/or rappellers. The amount of people in a load depends on the type of aircraft being used.
2. Retardant load. An aircraft will drop a retardant load on a fire to help slow the fire's spread.
3. Sling load. Cargo that is carried beneath a helicopter and attached by a long line and swivel.

Longline: A cable/wire line (at least 50 ft in length) that can be attached to the underside (belly) of a helicopter, for use in picking up and dropping off cargo nets full of equipment in the field.

Long-Range Spotting: Firebrands can travel long distances away from the fire, creating new fire starts. Firebrands can easily travel 1/4 mile or more, from the main fire.

Lookout:

1. A person designated to detect and report fires from a

lookout tower.

2. A location from which fires can be detected and reported.

3. A fire crewmember assigned to observe the fire from a vantage point and warn crewmembers when there is potential danger.

Manifest: A manifest is required for all flights to determine how much weight will be onboard. Passenger names are listed on the manifest as well as itemized cargo such as hazardous material. Qualified firefighters build flight manifests and present them to the pilot before take-off.

Manpurse: Most firefighters carry a "manpurse." It is a small Velcro organizer that can fit into a cargo pant pocket. A manpurse generally contains an IRPG, notepad, pen, sharpie, and Smokey calendar to keep track of hours worked.

Mark-3 Pump: A mark 3 pump is a portable pump that can be dropped to firefighters when a nearby water source is available.

MIST (Minimum Impact Suppression Tactics): A method of firefighting used to create minimal disturbance of the natural environment. MIST tactics are commonly used in designated wilderness areas.

Mock-Ups: Smokejumpers utilize mock-ups prior to an operational mission in an unfamiliar aircraft, while helicopter rappellers perform mock-ups in training. In either case, a mock-up allows the firefighter to have a "dry run" with the aircraft stationary on the ground in order to gain familiarity before going "live."

Moonscape: When a fire blankets thick gray ash on the forest floor for as far as the eye can see it is referred to as moonscape because it looks similar to being on the moon.

Mop-Up: After a fire has burned through an area, firefighters work the perimeter edges and/or the entire burned area (depending on the size of the fire) with hand tools -and sometimes water- to extinguish lingering pockets of heat. Mop-up is slow tedious work for firefighters.

MRE (Meal Ready to Eat): MREs are prepackaged meals, which were originally developed for the military to help meet the need of an extended shelf life and high-calorie content.

Natural Barrier: Any natural feature on the landscape that lacks flammable material and/or can obstruct the fire's spread. May also be referred to as a "firebreak."

Needle Cast: Pine needles that have been shed from trees.

New Start: New wildfire.

NICC: National Incident Coordination Center.

NIFC: National Interagency Fire Center.

Nomex: Nomex is the fire-resistant material that fire pants and fire shirts are made of. Nomex is required to be worn when on the fireline.

NWCG: National Wildfire Coordinating Group.

Off-Season: The winter months in the U.S. are generally considered the off-season. Seasonal firefighters are laid-off during the winter months, while firefighters who are employed year-round try to take a vacation before it disappears. This is a government agency phenomenon called "use or lose," where vacation time has a time limit and then goes away.

Old Schools: When a firefighter refers to "old schools," they are talking about a pair of Nomex pants and/or a Nomex shirt, from the 1960s or 70s.

Ops (Operations):
1. The unit within the Incident Command System- Operations
2. The person heading the operations unit is referred to as Operations or Ops.
3. Operations. The functional act of doing something out on the fireline.

Ops Normal: Ops normal is generally used as sarcastic commentary about how things might be a complete mess, but messy is normal, and everyone is used to dealing with it.

Overhead: Overhead refers to the supervisors above you. Example: A crewmember's overhead would be the superintendent and foreman and/or crewboss and assistant crewboss.

Pack Out: Refers to how smokejumpers and/or rappellers get their gear off of a remote wildfire. Firefighters pack all their fire gear/supplies into large packout bags, then hike across the landscape to reach a feasible pick-up point. A standard pack-out bag weighs approximately 85-110 lbs.

Pack Out Bag: A large bag that firefighters pack fire gear/supplies in, so they can hike it out of the forest.

Pack Test: The required annual physical endurance test for all fireline personnel. There are variations of the pack test depending on designated functions. However, arduous duty firefighters are required to complete a 3-mile walk on flat ground within 45 minutes, while carrying 45 lbs on their person.

Parts of a Fire: There are generally five parts of a fire. The heel, the head, the right/left flanks, and the point of origin. The heel is the back, the head is the front, the right/left flanks are the sides, and the point of origin is where the fire started.

Perm: Permanently employed wildland firefighter.

PG Bag (Personal Gear Bag): The issued bag that is used by firefighters to store 14 days' worth of their personal belongings. Also sometimes referred to as a red bag.

P-Line: A shortcut access trail that firefighters may build to make travel to/from the fire's edge quicker and easier.

PLF (Parachute Landing Fall): A PLF is a skill set taught to smokejumpers to help prevent landing injuries.

Point of Origin: The spot where the fire started, which could have come from a lightning strike, a spark, arson, etc.

PPE (Personal Protective Equipment): Different tasks within firefighting require different components of PPE. For example, all firefighters are required to wear a helmet when out on the fireline, but only sawyers and swampers are required to wear saw chaps.

Prescribed Fire/Burn: A fire that is intentionally set in order to benefit the health of the forest and/or improve animal habitat. A written and approved prescribed fire plan must exist prior to ignition. Also called an RX burn.

Pre Po/Pre-position. When fire resources have been called to a geographic area with high fire danger due to the likelihood of new fire starts, it is referred to as a *pre-*

po assignment.

Pre-treat: The use of water, foam, or retardant along a fireline in advance of the fire.

PSE (Permanent-Seasonal Firefighter): A firefighter who gets retirement and benefits, but is laid off for one-to-four months each year.

Pulaski: A combination tool that can be used for digging, trenching, or chopping. Pulaskis are the most universally utilized tool on the fireline.

Quals: *Qualifications.* A person's fire qualifications are listed on their "red card." Quals are gained after a firefighter has taken the appropriate classes and successfully completed the "taskbook" associated with the qualification.

Rappeller: A Type 1 firefighter that is flown by helicopter to remote and difficult to reach fires, then inserted into the fire by rappelling down a rope from the helicopter.

Rappel Spot: The spot that has been designated by the spotter for the rappellers to land in.

Rate of Spread: The term rate of spread is relative to the growth of a fire's size. Firefighters usually reference how many chains per hour the fire is burning to give a frame of reference for the fire activity. *See* "chain" definition.

RB/RS: Rookie bro, and rookie sis are terms commonly used by smokejumpers in relation to the people that they went through rookie training with.

Ready Load: Refers to the group of firefighters who are first up on the rotation board for a fire. Smokejumpers and rappellers both operate from a rotation board and the ready load consists of the number of people that can fit with regard to the aircraft's capacity.

Re-burn: Small remote fires that are responded to by smokejumpers and/or rappellers are required to be put out 100% since remote fires cannot be patrolled later. If one of these remote fires is still holding any heat, there is potential for a *re-burn*, which means the same fire has started back up again. It's considered to be quite embarrassing to have a re-burn on one of your fires.

Ready Shack/Ready Room: The place where smokejumpers and/or rappellers stage their gear in a manner that makes it easier for them put on when the alarm sounds to respond to a fire.

Recon: To scout out ahead of fire resources. Firefighters regularly take recon flights to get an aerial view of a fire.

Red Card: A small pocket-sized card that wildland firefighters carry with them, which is essentially their license to fight fire. The red card lists which qualifications the firefighter is certified for, as well trainee status positions.

Red Flag Warning: A term used by fire weather forecasters to alert firefighters of a critical fire weather threat.

Refurb: *Refurb* usually refers to getting gear "fire ready" after it has been used.

RH (Relative Humidity): RH helps firefighters determine the prime burning hours of the day. Fires burn the easiest during points of the day when RH is at its lowest.

Repeater: A radio signal station that relays a transmission so the message can travel a further distance. Repeaters are open channels, which means the communication can be heard by an entire forest if they are scanning that repeater channel.

Resource Order: The official form that is used to order

resources to a fire. The resource (crew, engine, etc.) brings the resource order with them to the incident and use it to check in to the incident.

Retardant Drop: Fire retardant that is dropped from a plane or heli-tanker over portions of a fire to help calm the flames is called a retardant drop.

Rhino: A specially designed firefighting hand tool.

Rock Scree: A large boulder field typically on the side of a slope, that has no combustible fuel to catch fire.

Roll: Slang for fire assignment. A firefighter might say that they are "headed out on a *roll*," which means that they'll more than likely be gone for at least 14 days.

Rotation Board: Smokejumpers and rappellers list all their firefighters on a rotation board at the beginning of the season (usually by drawing numbers out of a hat) and everyone stays in that order for the duration of the fire season. It determines who is next up for a fire assign-ment. The *rotation board* is considered to hold your fate for the season, for better or worse.

Rotor Wash: The air turbulence that occurs under a hovering helicopter. Rotor wash can be so significant that it can break out tree branches, knock over small-diameter trees, kick up a significant amount of dust, and/or intensify fire activity.

Round: When a log is cut into smaller chunks, those chunks are referred to as *rounds*.

Running Saw: Using a chainsaw.

SA (Situational Awareness): A term that is commonly used in firefighting to promote constant observation of the situation as well as your surroundings in relation to potential hazards.

Saddle: A saddle-shaped depression along the ridgeline of a hill/mountain between two higher points.

Safety Zone: When fire activity becomes extreme firefighters may need to retreat to a safety zone. An area that has been pre-identified by firefighters as a place relatively free of combustible material, and large enough for firefighters to safely wait out the intensified fire behavior.

Saw Line: A wide swath in the forest, which is cut by a fire crew's sawyers, ahead of the crew's digging squad. Saw line removes brush/fuel to help slow the fire before it reaches the fireline.

Saw Team/Partner: A saw team could consist of two sawyers who take turns cutting with the chainsaw (usually cutting for a full fuel tank and then switching), while the other person acts as their swamper. Or the saw team could consist of one sawyer and one swamper.

Sawyer: A sawyer is a person who has been certified to operate a chainsaw. Sawyers have varying experience and training levels and are certified based on skill.

Seasonal: Seasonally employed firefighter.

Scope of Duty: Qualifications, experience level, and position title all play a factor in one's scope of duty. To be operating outside of your scope of duty signifies that you have not been adequately trained for that responsibility, and/or the circumstances surpass capacity. This can happen when a fire is growing rapidly and there is a need to transition to a more experienced IC. The acting IC can choose to continue in that capacity until the transition, or they can choose to disengage. Either is acceptable so long as the acting IC is still within their comfort zone.

Scratch Line: A very basic fireline that is used as an

emergency measure to check the spread of fire. Most often used when the fire is moving quickly and there aren't enough firefighters to staff the fire.

Secret Squirrel Channel: A secret squirrel channel is a radio frequency where the transmissions can only be heard between the members of one particular crew.

Shot Crew: *Hotshot crew.*

Sigg: A small fuel bottle that looks similar to a metal water bottle.

Six-Hour Watch: The long-held tradition for small remote wilderness fires was to put the fire completely out and then sit and watch it for 6 hours. If a smoke popped up during the *six-hour watch*, the watch would start over again. This helped ensure that a fire would not restart after firefighters had left it.

Sizes of Fires: Fires are categorized as Type 5 through 1 in reference to size. A Type 5 fire is the smallest and least complex, while a Type 1 fire is the largest and most complex.

Size-Up: Firefighters will *size-up* a fire by scouting around the perimeter and taking several factors into account for the best course of action before resources engage on the fire.

Skier's Left/Right: Generally used to describe a location when talking on the radio. Example: "The snag that needs to be flagged is downslope from your location by about 100 ft., skier's right."

Slash: Slash refers to heavy amounts of down debris on the forest floor. It could have been generated from weather events, logging operations, etc.

Slicked Off Black: Slicked off black refers to an area where the fire has completely consumed all vegetation.

Sling Load: Cargo carried beneath a helicopter and attached by a line and swivel.

Sling Psychrometer: A hand-operated instrument for obtaining wet and dry bulb temperature readings and, subsequently, relative humidity. Using this method is commonly referred to by firefighters as slinging weather, or spinning weather.

Slopover: When part of a fire crosses over the fireline where it was meant to keep from advancing, that is considered a *slopover*.

Smokejumper: A Type 1 firefighter that is flown by plane to remote and difficult to reach fires, then inserted into the fire by parachuting from an airplane.

Snag: A standing dead tree, burned or unburned. Snags present a hazard on the fireline and identifying them and/or removing them is important to firefighter safety.

Soup Sandwich: A term used to reference a person who is essentially a hot mess.

Spike Camp: A smaller, more primitive version of a fire camp that is set in a remote location. Spike camps are set up to lessen the commute time of firefighters to certain portions of the fire. Spike camps generally provide food, water, and some basic supplies. A spike camp can also consist of one single crew and very basic provisions, such as MREs, drinking water, and chainsaw fuel. When this is the case, it's referred to as spiking out.

Spiked Out: When a fire resource sleeps on/very near

the fire's edge with very little logistical support.

Spooled Up: When a helicopter's rotors are turning while it is sitting on the ground, it's considered *spooled-up* and ready to go. This saying can also refer to someone's attitude. "They got all *spooled-up* about it!"

Spot Fire: A small fire that starts up outside the main fire due to a firebrand crossing over the fireline into receptive fuels.

Spotter: A person who is charged with designating a jump or rappel spot, interacting with the pilot, and sending jumpers or rappellers out of their respective aircraft through hand signals and/or verbal commands.

Spotter Check: A safety gear check performed by a spotter before a live operation.

Spotting:
1. When firebrands from the main fire are carried by the wind, land in unburned fuel, and ignite new smaller fires, that is referred to as *spotting*. Spot fires can vary greatly in size.
2. When jumpers or rappellers load up and fly off to respond to an initial attack fire, the spotter would be

considered to be "spotting a load."

Spur Ridge: Topographically, there are "main ridges" that are essentially the spine or backbone of a mountain. A spur ridge is a small off-chute of the main ridgeline. There are generally several spur ridges on any one mountain.

Squad: Usually made up of 5-7 people. A crew of 20 people breaks down into smaller squads, each with their own respective squad leader.

Squaddie: *Squad leader.*

Squad Boss: *Squad leader.* The supervisor of 5-7 people when the larger crew gets split up for work assignments.

Stable vs. Unstable Atmosphere: In relation to firefighting, fires burn hotter and with more intensity when the atmosphere is unstable and you can expect poor visibility due to smoke when the atmosphere is stable.

Staff Ride: A valuable learning tool where firefighters visit the location of a fatality fire to get a clearer understanding of what happened. Typically, some firefighters who were directly involved in the incident attend in order to provide students of fire with first-hand knowledge.

Staging: *See:* Pre-Po and Staging Area.

Staging Area: A geographical location where fire resources are placed to wait for their assignment.

Stick: "A Stick" refers to two people exiting an aircraft together. Smokejumpers exit the aircraft in *sticks,* as do helicopter rappellers.

Superintendent (Supt): The highest-ranking person on a hotshot crew.

Sup: Short for the title of Supervisor. Example: I just talked to the Forest Sup and she said...

Swamper: A swamper is a person who works with a sawyer to help them clear away brush and debris as they cut and buck trees.

Switchback: Sometimes hiking trails are built where they essentially zig zag back and forth up a slope. Switchbacks are used to help lessen the effort to reach the top when a slope is steep.

Swivel: A metal hook that swivels in either direction. It's used to configure the long line for transporting sling loads of cargo by helicopter.

Taskbook: In order for any firefighter to become certified for fire qualifications they must first complete the tasks within the taskbook for that specific qualification. Generally, each task (of which there are several in any one taskbook) needs to be performed competently three times before being "signed off."

Team: Short for incident management team (IMT). An IMT comes to take control of a fire when it has grown past the capacity of local resources to manage.

TFR (Temporary Flight Restriction): A TFR is a restricted airspace placed over a wildfire, and put into effect by the Federal Aviation Administration (FAA). The restriction is requested by fire officials so that nonessential aircraft don't fly into the airspace above a fire. TFRs protect fire pilots from potentially crashing with civilian aircraft.

The Black: "The black" is the area that a wildfire has already burned through. It could be referred to as clean black if the fire consumed everything cleanly, or skunky/ dirty black if the fire left vegetation that could catch fire again later.

The Green: "The green" refers to areas that have not been burned. The green is what firefighters are trying to protect. If firefighters were performing a grid search for spot fires they would be walking through *the green.*

Thermal Belt: A geographic area, usually toward the upper third of a mountain, where the temperatures stay relatively warm throughout the night, rather than cooling down.

Tied-In: The act of connecting one section of fireline to another section of fireline or natural barrier. Oftentimes multiple fire resources are working simultaneously on different portions of the fire and work until they meet one another, essentially, tying in the line. Firefighters also tie in with one another to have a conversation or to come up with a plan.

Torching: When a single tree or a small group of trees catch fire in a flaring fashion, after being cured to burn by the surrounding ground fire.

TU (Tits Up): When somebody "goes down" on the fireline from overexertion or heat stress, firefighters say the person went TU.

Travel Pants: Most fire crews are required to travel home from a fire assignment in "clean greens." They are referred to as travel pants because firefighters will only wear them on their travel home. Because of this, firefighters might use old school Nomex pants as their travel pants, because they are too delicate to wear on the fireline but very comfortable.

Two More Chains: A chain is a measure of distance. A firefighter might ask how much further they have to go until they tie in the fireline they are building. The answer they get will probably be, "two more chains," meaning we aren't there yet, but we're getting close. Of course, it's never only two more chains.

Type: Refers to resource capability. A Type 1 resource might provide more power, size, capacity, qualifications, etc.; than would be found with a Type 2 resource. Resource typing helps standardize fire equipment and resources, which makes it easier for people to understand what they are ordering.

UAS (Unmanned Aircraft System): *Also known as drones.* Wildland firefighters use drones in multiple ways in assistance of fire operations.

UB (Union Break): Someone might say they are taking a UB when they sit down and grab a snack.

Underburn: A fire that consumes surface fuels but not the overstory canopy in a forest.

Underslung Line: A fireline that is placed below a fire that is burning on a slope. Underslung line can present several problems due to the potential that burning material might roll out, below the fire, starting a new fire further down the hill.

Use-or-Lose: A term referring to time off. Many firefighters don't have the luxury of taking time off during the year so their vacation hours accumulate. The government will take those hours away if they aren't used by a certain date, so firefighters tend to "burn" their use-or- lose in November and December before it disappears.

Virga: Precipitation falling out of a cloud, that evaporates before it reaches the ground.

Water Tender: A ground vehicle which transports large volumes of water to strategic locations. Water tenders may also be used to dampen down very dusty areas prior to helicopters landing/taking-off, etc.

Wet Line: A line of water, or water/chemical retardant, that gets sprayed along the ground to act as a temporary control line. It can help to slow a fire down temporarily.

Widowmaker: A portion of a tree/limb that is stuck in the branches of another tree. The fact that it could fall out at any time, potentially killing a person, is why it is called a widowmaker.

Wildfire Module (WFM): Wildfire Mods are versatile fire resources that assist with prescribed fire preparation and execution, managing wildfires for resource benefit, fuels reduction work, wildfire response, etc.

Windfall/Windrow: Trees knocked over or broken off by the wind; also, sometimes called blowdown. Large areas of dense blowdown can create a serious fire hazard.

Work-to-Rest: A phrase that speaks to the amount of rest required for each hour worked. Current NWCG guidelines require one hour of rest for every two hours in work status. The average shift for a firefighter is 16 hours with 8 hours off.

Yard Sale: Generally, firefighters are pretty dialed, and organized because space is limited in vehicles, fire packs, etc. When a person has their stuff all over the place fellow firefighters refer to it as a yard sale and might offer them some money for a couple of their items just to give them a hard time.

Yellow: When a firefighter refers to their yellow, they are talking about their fire-resistant button-up fire shirt. Although fire shirts have been yellow for almost the entire history of wildland firefighting, there are fire shirts in other colors. Ironically, people still refer to their fire shirt as their "yellow" whether it's yellow or not.

Volume Bravo Contributors

Julian Affuso- Déjà vu

Life Advice: Seek harmony, not balance. Harmony, if you can find it, will feel like a symphony. The key is that your actions are in harmony with all other parts of your life.

Fire Advice: Always truly understand the WHY. If you do, and you believe in the WHY, you can accomplish anything.

Leona Allen- 'Booker' (Artwork)

Life Advice: Respecting nature is respecting yourself.

Fire Advice: Communicate, hydrate, and leave your ego behind.

Quin Anderson- The Sharp Rock Fire

Kate Averett- Weathered, The Digs, Seasoned

Life/Fire Advice: Don't forget to have fun.

Hanne Beener- The Horse

Life advice: Multitasking is rarely worth it if you can avoid it. Also, get up early.

Fire Advice: Take any opportunity to explore your surroundings.

Betsy Booth- September 3 at 8402'

Fire Advice: Hear advice and correction; and perhaps more importantly, give it in the spirit of leveling-up the crew, the incident, the forest, whatever. Try and bring the whole dang thing up to its highest potential. Even if someone is being a dick about it, take what applies in this spirit, and then forget the leftovers and the dickishness (And try not to be the dick).

BMEL- Watch This

Life Advice: Strength begins from within. Do you have self trust?

Fire Advice: If you ARE ready you don't have to GET ready.

Sarah Brown- Chapter 2 Opening Quote

Life Advice: Pay Attention.

Fire Advice: Those people you meet on the fireline- Those are your people, for all of time.

Chase Burgett- Helicopter (Artwork)

Fire Advice: Earn it every day!

Rita Chandler- Angel in Whites

Life Advice: Accept advice graciously- you may not want it today; but you may need it tomorrow.

Fire Advice: Pay attention.

Echo Cunningham- Salt//Ash

Life Advice: It's time to start living by your own clock.

Fire Advice: Everything works if you let it.

Marissa Duarte- Engine 414 (Artwork)

Life Advice: What you have is meant for you while you have it.

Fire Advice: Suck it up.

Riva Duncan- Attention!

Life Advice: Wear sunscreen.

Fire Advice: Always fight for your people and put them first.

Chris Hensley- More Fire on the Landscape (Artwork)

Life Advice: Learn to live with intention while embracing imperfection. Be a seeker of knowledge, inexorably in passion.

Fire Advice: Take time off. Seriously! Take. Time. Off.

Sy Holmes- The Things We Hauled Around On The Bus

Taylor Kress- Summer's Ending

Danna Lusk- Anchor and Flank Candles

Life Advice: My dad once told me, "Remember: No matter where you go...there you are." At first, I thought it was dumb but now I know he's a genius.

Fire Advice: To all the dispatchers out there; you're the calm in the chaos. Keep it cool, fool!

Andrew Mattox: The Few, the Proud, the Lost

Life advice: When confronting your failings, remember that we've all got to harass the universe somehow.

Fire Advice: Don't stand under helicopters. And never play cards with a man whose name starts with a city.

Courtney McGee- Saw Shutdown, Naked People, Chapter 5 Opening Quote

Life advice: Life is made up of peaks and valleys. We wouldn't know what peaks are without valleys.

Fire advice: One of my crew bosses once told me "you've got to know when to hold them and know when to fold them."

Willow Merritt- Miserable Fun

Life advice: Stop worrying about what others think about you and start living your life, you'll be much happier in the long run.

Fire Advice: Slow is smooth and smooth is fast.

Ian Morgan- Division Wake-Up

Life/Fire Advice: Don't take love advice from a hotshot.

The Evolving Nomad- I Know This Place

Life advice: You'll never be younger than you are right now, and you might not have a tomorrow. Live life accordingly.

Fire Advice: Work smarter, not harder.

Bre Orcasitas- The Mosaic, Substandard House Guest, The Firefighter in the Meadow, Rookie Van

Life Advice: If you want to feel content in life, be in rhythm with nature.

Fire Advice: Go slow to go fast.

Forest E. Ployer- First Fire

Fire Advice: Don't just stovepipe your red card in operations. Always be a student of fire.

D.B. Robbins - Pastime Leather Co.

Life Advice: Ask God to move a mountain, but be ready to wake up to a shovel.

Fire Advice: When shit is hitting the fan, fall back to the basics of firefighting. One foot in the black.

Brent Ruby- Haunted by Samples

Issak Sager- Yep, We're on a Fire. It's Hot.

Life/Fire Advice: Saying I don't know something, has gotten me further in life than pretending I do. The sooner you do that, the faster you really learn.

Gifford Sikorsky- Cup Trench

Life Advice: Take available opportunities.

Fire Advice: You might be lucky enough to get maximum SA in the form of a helicopter ride to your fire, but that's useless if you forget to GPS your helispot, camp, or the fire itself.

Will Silverman- Fire Floe

Life Advice: Appreciate each moment and try to live in the present.

Fire Advice: Respect the power of fire. Though fire provides awesome displays, it can also take your life in a heartbeat.

Jamie Strelnik- My Last Supper

Fire Advice: Be the last to sit down, be the first stand, always volunteer, and be a learner.

Sara Sweeney- Mimbres Memories, Nightshift in Willow Creek , Polles Fire

Life/Fire Advice: Be kind, be humble, kick ass.

Sheena Waters- (Artwork) Bull Elk, Bridger Teton

Jessica Westbrook- Out with a Boo!

Life Advice: Take care of your health, but also eat that slice of pie if it takes care of your happiness!

Fire Advice: This job is too serious to be taken so seriously all of the time. Do good work and be safe, but remember to have fun!

Acknowledgements

This is the section where the truth comes out. It's the space to reflect back on what it took to publish this book, and the people who made it possible.

Whitney Tayer is one of the people to which I owe a debt of gratitude. She's a fantastic no-nonsense proofreader who is as equally loyal to the written word as she is to honoring the idiosyncrasies of fire language. Thank you, Whitney!

James McGury. Without James this book would not be what it is. I've learned that a creative partnership is formed when neither person has the entire vision or skillset all their own, but together they can turn concept into reality. Thank you, James for your dedication to this project. You'll forever remain one of my favorite people to receive emails from because there's almost always an exciting attachment to open!

Beyond creative partnerships, there are also life partnerships. The people in our daily lives who we run ideas past, and seek advice from. The ones who support our efforts, root for us, listen to our rants, and remind us about the aspects of life that actually matter. To my family, my fire family, and my friend family, I love you fiercely. Thank you for meandering through this lifetime with me; your company makes all the difference.

And lastly, I'd like to thank each of the contributors from both volumes of *Hold and Improve*. Your willingness to share your stories and talents is what brings these books to life, and helps to preserve the fire culture for future generations.

The *Hold and Improve* Series

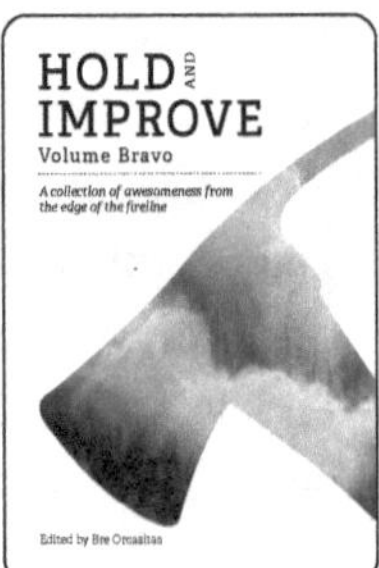

Scan this QR code for information about how to make a
submission for future volumes of *Hold and Improve,*
or visit: *www.thevolvingnomad.com*